ON THE TRAIL WITH

John
the Apostle

ON THE TRAIL WITH

John
the Apostle

DAILY DEVOTIONAL
READINGS

Lon Eckdahl

EQUIP
PRESS

ON THE TRAIL WITH

John the Apostle

Copyright © 2021 Lon Eckdahl

All rights reserved. No part of this publication may be reproduced, distributed, or transmitted in any form or by any means, without prior written permission.

Published by Equip Press, Colorado Springs, CO

Scripture quotations marked (NIV) are taken from the Holy Bible, New International Version. Copyright © 1973, 1978, 1984, 2011 by Biblica, Inc.® Used by permission. All rights reserved worldwide.

Scripture quotations marked (NRSV) are taken from the New Revised Standard Version Bible, copyright © 1989 the Division of Christian Education of the National Council of the Churches of Christ in the United States of America. Used by permission. All rights reserved.

First Edition: 2021
On the Trail with John the Apostle / Lon Eckdahl
Paperback ISBN: 978-1-951304-56-0
eBook ISBN: 978-1-951304-57-7

Acknowledgments

I would like to acknowledge and thank two very special ladies. First of all my wife, who has been extremely supportive of the book. I would also like to thank Sharon Schuur who did the proofreading and who made numerous suggestions that made the manuscript much better. God bless them both! And I especially want to thank my brother, Larry Eckdahl, for his wonderful support of this project.

Introduction

The attempt of this devotional book is to create a type of hike through the Gospel of John. Whenever we hike through different kinds of terrain it usually involves hills and valleys with all types of vistas along the way. This will be true as we hike through John's Gospel. There are valleys and there are mountain tops. There are places where we can sit for a while and take in the scenery. And along the way we will become acquainted with the Apostle himself. Now, on this hike it is important that you take your Bible, and a heart that is open to whatever God wants to show you.

This is not a 365-day devotional book. Rather it is a journey that ends when we get to the end of John's Gospel! And even though it is laid out day by day, you might take two or three days just to meditate in one particular spot. On some days the scriptural portion is longer than others; on those days I have asked you to read the selected portion in your own Bible. The translation I will be using throughout the journey is the New International Version.

John was a fisherman along with his brother James. The fishing business was a rugged business. There were many frustrating nights when the brothers caught nothing. They experienced many a storm on the Sea of Galilee. But one day their lives were changed. A man they had never seen before walked into their world. He spoke like no one had ever spoken. And lo and behold, He invited them to follow Him. Why would these fishermen leave everything they knew to follow this itinerant preacher?

APPLICATION:

Have you ever heard the call of Jesus to follow Him? Did you respond in the positive? And if so, how has your choice to follow Him affected your life? As we take this hike through the Gospel of John I think you will see why John, and others, made the choice to follow this One called Jesus.

VERSE TO MEMORIZE:

I Peter 2:21

Day 1

The Delayed Preface

At the beginning of many books is a preface, or the beginning remarks of what the book is about or the intended purpose of the book. John also writes a preface in his gospel, but it's not at the beginning; it's at the end. In chapter 20:30-31 John writes: **"Jesus did many other miraculous signs in the presence of His disciples, which are not recorded in this book. But these are written that you may believe that Jesus is the Christ, the Son of God, and that by believing you may have life in His name."**

John did not write his gospel to give us an historical account. Nor did he write to tell us a bunch of stories about all he experienced in his walk with Jesus. John had a specific purpose for writing. He wrote what he wrote with one purpose in mind: that those who read what he wrote would come to faith. He wants us to believe with all of our hearts that Jesus is the Christ, the Son of the living God. And when we believe the result will be eternal life.; eternal life is not quantity of years, but quality of life!

APPLICATION:

Faith is not something you have, it is something you do! What we really believe effects how we live our lives. When I truly believe in Jesus, my life should reflect that belief in every activity I do, and every decision I make.

VERSES TO MEMORIZE:

John 20:30-31

Day 2

John 1:1-2

**"In the beginning was the Word,
and the Word was with God,
and the Word was God.
He was with God in the beginning."**

When Moses recorded the genesis of all things, he started by saying, **"In the beginning God created the heavens and the earth." (Genesis 1:1)** John begins his gospel at the same place – the beginning! In talking about the Godhead, John tells us that not only was the Word with God, the Word was God!

As we go on in the creation story we meet the third Person of the Godhead, the Holy Spirit, for Moses goes on to write, **"Now the earth was formless and empty, darkness was over the surface of the deep, and the Spirit of God was hovering over the waters."** Then the creative agent of the Godhead begins to add dimension to His creation: **"And

God said, Let there be light." And God said, Let there be water." "And God said, Let there be vegetation." And it goes on from there.

The key words are: **"And God said."** God's Word was the creative agent of the Godhead. God spoke the world into existence. John picks up on that when he writes,

> **"Through Him all things were made;
> without Him nothing was made that has
> been made."**

Our words are an extension of our being. It is by our words that others come to know us. Our words are vital to who we are. Jesus was **"the Word become flesh."** (1:14).

APPLICATION:

What do your words say about you? Do they reflect what and who you really are? Your own words can also be creative. Your words can create or change the atmosphere around you. Use them wisely.

VERSE TO MEMORIZE:
John 1:14

Day 3

John 1:4-5

**"In Him was life, and that life
was the light of men.
The light shines in the darkness,
but the darkness has not understood it."**

This is a real mountaintop passage! John tells us that in Jesus there is life. And Jesus, in His own words says in John 10:10, **"I have come that they may have life, and have it to the full."** In other words, when we enter into a relationship with Jesus Christ, it is His will that we experience a full and meaningful life. Someone separated from Christ has no idea what genuine life really is.

Not only does God want us, as His children, to experience true life, He also tells us that this life is the light of men. Now what does light do? It distills the darkness; it reveals what is around us. And Jesus, as the light, reveals to us what God is really like. He helps us to see things like He sees them. Light exposes evil and enhances righteousness.

John goes on to tell us that this **"light shines in the darkness, but the darkness has not understood it."** The New Living Translation puts it this way: **"The light shines in the darkness, and the darkness can never extinguish it."** The darkness can never extinguish the light, but light will always extinguish the darkness. You can walk into a pitch-dark room, and light a candle or turn on a flashlight, and the darkness will be immediately eliminated.

APPLICATION:

Are you a bearer of the light? Are you allowing the light of Christ to shine brightly through your life? Jesus said, **"Let your light shine before men, that they may see your good deeds and praise your Father in heaven."** (Matt. 5:16)

VERSE TO MEMORIZE:

Matthew 5:16

Day 4

John 1:6-9

**"There came a man who was sent from God;
his name was John.
He came as a witness to testify
concerning that light,
so that through him all men might believe.
He himself was not the light; he came only as a
witness to the light.
The true light that gives light to every man
was coming into the world."**

Now John introduces another John; John the Baptist. He tells us that John the Baptist was actually sent from God. In other words, he came with a definite purpose in mind. He came to be the forerunner of the Christ, the Messiah. And as the forerunner he was to give witness to the Light, the Light that was Jesus. And what was his ultimate goal? That all men might believe!

John makes it clear that John the Baptist was not THE LIGHT; he only came to give witness to the Light. For the

Bible makes it clear that Jesus was the "TRUE LIGHT" that in essence gives light to every man and woman. God does not hide from us! His purpose is that we might come to know Him! And how do we come to know Him? By acknowledging Him through His creation; through His Word; and through the witness of others who have come to know Him.

The Apostle Paul makes it clear in Romans 1:20 when he says, **"For since the creation of the world God's invisible qualities – His eternal power and divine nature – have been clearly seen, being understood from what He has made, so that men are without excuse."**

APPLICATION:

Are you aware that God in His wisdom has made Himself known in so many ways? Have you really developed an awareness of what His creation shows us? Have you read His Word? Have you felt the power of His Holy Spirit wooing you to Himself? And have you listened to the testimonies of His people? The Bible talks about those who intentionally allow themselves to become blind and deaf to the Truth of God's Word. I trust that isn't you!

VERSE TO MEMORIZE:

Romans 1:20

Day 5

John 1:10-11

**"He was in the world, and though the world
was made by Him,
the world did not recognize Him.
He came to that which was His own,
but His own did not receive Him."**

These two verses are all about rejection. John is writing about Jesus, and the fact that God's Son, the creative agent of the Godhead, has come into the world He Himself created but was rejected by that world. There are so many ways that a person can be rejected, or even feel rejection. It is such an empty, haunting feeling if you have ever experienced it. Jesus loved this world more than we will ever comprehend, and yet that which He loved turned away from Him.

There is a poem entitled "Indifference" written by Geoffrey Studdert Kennedy which helps define what rejection feels like.

When Jesus came to Golgotha,
they hanged Him on a tree.
They drove great nails through hands and feet,
and made a Calvary.
They crowned Him with a crown of thorns,
red were His wounds and deep.
For those were crude and cruel days,
and human flesh was cheap.

When Jesus came to Birmingham,
they simply passed Him by.
They would not hurt a hair of Him,
they only let Him die.
For men had grown more tender,
and they would not give Him pain.
They only passed down the street,
and left Him in the rain.

Still Jesus cried, "Forgive them,
for they know not what they do."
And still it rained the winter rain
that drenched Him through and through.
The crowds went home and left the streets
without a soul to see.
And Jesus crouched against a wall,
and cried for Calvary.

APPLICATION:

Rejection is an awful thing! And yet so many of us have rejected Jesus at one time or another. If you have rejected Him in your heart, maybe you ought to ask for His forgiveness and let Him fill you with His divine love. After all, He died to forgive you!

VERSE TO MEMORIZE:
Hebrews 12:25

Day 6

John 1:12-13

**"But to all who received Him,
to those who believed in His name,
He gave the right to become children of God—
children born not of natural descent,
nor of human decision
or a husband's will, but born of God."**

We have a choice: to reject or to embrace! Oh, the joy of embracing the One who gave His life for you and me. John says here that to believe and place our trust in Jesus is to become a child of God. We are adopted into His wonderful family. As a pastor for over fifty years I have come to love the Family of God. They are the ones I plan to spend eternity with! Remember Jesus' words to Nicodemus: **"No one can see the Kingdom of God unless he is born again." (John 3:3)**

It is not a natural birth as John says here: it is a spiritual birth. More about that later when we get to John, chapter three.

Notice John also says here, **"He gave the right to become children of God."** What gave us the right? The fact that God's Son came to our world and gave His life for our sin on an old rugged cross. Like the old hymn says, "Jesus paid it all, all to Him I owe, sin had left a crimson stain; He washed it white as snow." My right to become His child is based on nothing I have done, but on everything He has done. Praise God for the truth of that statement!

APPLICATION:

Are you His child today? Are you part of His wonderful family? Have you taken advantage of the "right" He gave you when He sent Jesus to die in your place? It's really so easy: confess to Him your sinfulness; ask Him to forgive you and to take up residence in your heart; and then go forth to serve Him to the best of your ability.

VERSE TO MEMORIZE:

John 3:16

Day 7

John 1:14

**"The Word became flesh
and made His dwelling among us.
We have seen His glory,
the glory of the One and Only,
who came from the Father,
full of grace and truth."**

Here is another mountain peak in our hike through John's gospel. The Word, the creative Agent of the Godhead, became flesh and made His dwelling among us. WOW! Do you realize everything that is in that statement? The Divine Son of God, the One Person of the Trinity God used to speak our world into existence. He became flesh!! He became one of us. And not only that, He made the decision to dwell among us!

How did it happen? Well, you've heard of Christmas, the day we celebrate His coming into our world. This is the only place that John even alludes to the reality of Christmas. This is John's Christmas statement. Jesus came, and He chose to live among us, and as He did we beheld His glory. It is a glory full of grace and truth.

The story of Jesus' coming is indeed the greatest story ever told! He came to our world in the very same way we came to this world – He was born as a baby! And surprise of surprises, He was born in a stable, with the animals. Now, if you don't think it was the surprise of the ages, then there are some shepherds I would like for you to talk to!

Somebody once asked me, "Why was Jesus born in a stable?" And then they said, "Because that's where all of the sacrifices were born!" You see, Jesus came to fulfill the Old Testament prophecy of the "Sacrificial Lamb" that would come into our world.

And what does it mean, He was "full of grace and truth?" There is an acrostic for grace = **G**od's **R**iches **A**t **C**hrist's **E**xpense. Grace is God's unmerited favor freely offered to us. We can't do anything to earn it – it's God's free gift to us! And truth is the opposite of falsehood. Our God knows nothing but Truth. Jesus said, **"I am the Way, the Truth and the Life."** He is all of that and more!

APPLICATION:

Have you reached out to embrace God's Christmas gift to you? He is all you will ever need. But without Him, nothing you have will be enough.

VERSE TO MEMORIZE:
Romans 6:23

Day 8

John 1:15-18

"John testifies concerning Him.
He cries out, saying,
'This was He of whom I said,
He who comes after me has surpassed me
because He was before me.'
From the fullness of His grace
we have all received one blessing after another.
For the law was given through Moses;
grace and truth came through Jesus Christ.
No one has ever seen God,
but God the One and Only,
who is at the Father's side,
has made Him known."

"John testifies concerning Him." In other words, John the Baptist testifies concerning Jesus! This man sent from God, John the Baptist, came as a forerunner of the Christ. He came to bring an awareness of what God was about to do in the sending of His Son. Jesus came to deal a death blow to sin. John was preaching a message of repentance, that all men should turn from their sin and seek the righteousness of Almighty God.

Now the Apostle makes it clear that John the Baptist is superior to him because of the unique work God the Father has given him. In John the Baptist we have seen the uniqueness of God's grace and truth. Every blessing we have received comes from God's grace and truth. Even though we have never seen God, when Jesus came, God made Himself known to us. In John 14:9 Jesus said to Philip, **"Anyone who has seen Me has seen the Father."**

Consider the difference between God's grace and His mercy. Grace is that which God gives us that we do not deserve. Mercy is what God withholds from us that we do deserve. And we definitely need both His mercy and His grace!

APPLICATION:
I want you to have the assurance today that in Christ we have been given access to God's bank account of grace and truth!

VERSES TO MEMORIZE:
John 14:6-7

Day 9

Read – John 1:19-28

This is a little longer passage, so I want you to look it up and read it in your own Bible. You see, John the Baptist was really the last of the Old Testament prophets. And he was unique in every way: the way he dressed, where he lived, and what he ate. And because of his unique lifestyle and message, he drew a lot of attention.

The leaders of Judaism confronted him about who he was. They asked him if he was the Christ, or if he was Elijah come back, or if he was a prophet. John answered "No" to all of these suggestions. Then they said, "Tell us who you are!" And John answered, **"I am the voice of one calling in the desert, 'Make straight the way for the Lord.'"** These are direct words from the prophet Isaiah in Isaiah 40:3.

The next question they asked him was, "Then why are you baptizing?" And John answered, **"I baptize with water unto**

repentance, but there is One coming after me and He is the One you really want to see. I am not even worthy to untie His sandals." With all of the attention John the Baptist received, he immediately pointed the people to Jesus.

APPLICATION:

Does your life point people to Jesus? We love it when we receive a little attention from those around us, but our mission is not about us; it's about Him. Oh, that we would spend our days pointing people to Jesus!

VERSE TO MEMORIZE:

Revelation 12:11

Day 10

John 1:29-31

**"The next day John saw Jesus
coming toward him and said,
"Look, the Lamb of God,
who takes away the sin of the world!
This is the One I meant when I said,
A man who comes after me
has surpassed me because He was before me.
I myself did not know Him,
but the reason I came baptizing with water
was that He might be revealed to Israel."**

I think it is interesting that John the Baptist knew beyond a shadow of a doubt that Jesus came to deal a death blow to the sin issue. Our God is repulsed by the sin in our lives. Sin is what separates us from a loving heavenly Father. That's why, in His great love, He sent Jesus to be the supreme sacrifice for our sin. The blood of bulls and goats would no longer suffice, we needed something greater than that.

So, the very next day, when John saw Jesus, he said to his own disciples, **"Look, there He is, the Lamb of God who takes away the sin of the world!"** John is still pointing others to Jesus! Then, in essence, John says, "The reason I am doing what I am doing is so the world will come to know Him."

APPLICATION:

I wish we were all focused on our mission as much as John the Baptist was focused on his. The Great Commission given to us by Jesus is that we would be His witnesses. Like John, we are to point others to Jesus!

VERSES TO MEMORIZE:
Colossians 1:28-29

Day 11

John 1:32-34

**"Then John gave this testimony:
I saw the Spirit come down
from heaven as a dove and remain on Him.
I would not have known Him,
except the One who sent me
to baptize with water told me,
'The man on whom you see the Spirit
come down and remain is
He who will baptize with the Holy Spirit.'
I have seen and I testify that this is
the Son of God."**

When John the Baptist first saw Jesus, he did not recognize Him as God's Son, the Messiah sent down to the earth. It was only after God the Father identified Him as such by sending the Holy Spirit, in the form of a dove, to identify Him. This whole event may be hard to understand, but if you have ever had God speak to you or direct you in some unique way, then you know exactly what I am talking about. God doesn't speak audibly, but He does have a way of identifying His will for our lives. He has a unique way of leading us in discovering His divine will for us through the Holy Spirit whom He has given to us.

The dove, through scripture, has often been a symbol of the Holy Spirit. And even though Jesus was a cousin to John, John says, "I would not have known Him, except." To "know Jesus" in scripture, is to have a personal experience with Him. You may have been raised in the church, or born into a Christian family, or the fact you live in what has been called a Christian nation, yet if you do not have a personal relationship with Him, then you really don't know Him! And just like John, it is the Holy Spirit who really introduces us to Jesus. He places conviction on our hearts that this truly is the Son of God who gave His life on an old rugged cross that we might be forgiven of our sins, and that we might really "know Him."

APPLICATION:

So the question I ask you is, "Do you really know Him? Are you in an intimate relationship with Him? And if so, how has it changed your life?"

VERSE TO MEMORIZE:

John 17:3

Day 12

Read – John 1:35-42

Here we have the story of Jesus calling two of John the Baptist's disciples to be His disciples, one being Andrew. The other is thought to be John himself. As these two disciples are walking with John the Baptist, John spots Jesus, and identifies Him as the **"Lamb of God."** They immediately begin to follow Jesus. Now Jesus became aware that these two were following Him, so He turned and asked them, **"What do you want?"**

That is really a very good question! If you have taken any interest at all in knowing who Jesus is, then the question is offered to you, "What do you want? What are you looking for? What do you really want Jesus to do for you?"

Their answer is also quite unique. Their response to Jesus question was, **"Where are You staying?"** That sounds like someone who really doesn't know what to ask. So Jesus responds, **"Come and see."** For me, this whole conversation is very eye-opening. Where does Jesus stay? Even today, where does Jesus want to reside? He wants to reside in our heart. He wants to make His abode in our lives. In fact, He really wants to take His position on the throne of our lives. He not only wants to be our Savior, He also wants to be our Lord!

And so, Andrew (and supposedly John), spent the rest of that day with Jesus. When the day ended, Andrew couldn't wait to get home to tell his brother. Andrew becomes the very first evangelist in the New Testament. Andrew says to his brother Peter, **"We have found the Messiah, the Christ!"** Then Andrew takes Peter to Jesus. Andrew doesn't just tell Peter about Jesus, he takes him to Him. No better form of witnessing has ever been discovered: to tell others about Jesus, then to introduce them to Him personally! We need a whole lot more Andrews in the Church!

APPLICATION:

Well, you have probably already guessed what the application is. Be an evangelist; tell others about the Christ; then introduce them to Him. The enthusiasm people see in our own lives is really the key element!

VERSES TO MEMORIZE:
Matthew 28:18-20

Day 13

Read – John 1:43-50

John has introduced us to some of the people who are very special to him. We have met John the Baptist, Jesus, Andrew and his brother Peter. In this passage we meet Philip and Nathaniel. When it comes to Philip, it seems Jesus was actually looking for him. In verse 43 it says, **"Finding Philip, Jesus said to him, 'Follow Me.'"**

Now there is no suggestion that Philip delayed his response to Jesus' words. He immediately followed. In fact, as soon as he could, Philip shared with his friend Nathaniel that he had found the One Moses had written about, the One referred to as Jesus of Nazareth. Now Nathaniel didn't have much respect for anyone from Nazareth. Nazareth was considered kind of like the town on the other side of the tracks. So he responds to Philip, **"Can anything good come from there?" And Philip responded with the same words Jesus used when He called Andrew and John, "Come and see!"**

Jesus was impressed when he first saw Nathaniel. Jesus said, **"Here is a true Israelite, in whom there is nothing false."** Nathaniel was truly a man of integrity. A man of his word. A man who spoke the truth. But when Jesus said these words Nathaniel responded, **"How do You know me?"** Jesus had never seen Nathaniel before Philip took him to Jesus. When Nathaniel realized that Jesus had seen clear through him, he responded, **"Rabbi, You are the Son of God; You are the King of Israel." And Jesus responded, "You haven't seen anything yet. You are actually going to see angels ascending and descending on the Son of Man."** (paraphrase)

APPLICATION:

Do you understand just how well God knows every one of us? Someone once said to me, "God knows exactly what it's like to be you!" God knows you through and through. He knows why you do what you do. He understands the temptations you have trouble with. How does such knowing affect how you choose to live your life?

VERSES TO MEMORIZE:
John 2:24-25

Day 14

John 2:1-5

"On the third day a wedding took place
at Cana in Galilee.
Jesus' mother was there,
and Jesus and His disciples had also
been invited to the wedding.
When the wine was gone,
Jesus' mother said to Him,
'They have no more wine.'
'Dear woman, why do you involve Me?
My time has not yet come.'
His mother said to the servants,
'Do whatever He tells you.'"

I know it's kind of odd to go to a wedding in the middle of a hike, but this is a very important wedding. It is the occasion for Jesus' very first miracle. The wedding must have been for some members of Jesus' extended family, because of the fact that He and His disciples were invited. Also, there's the fact that Jesus' mother felt some responsibility when the wine ran out—why do you think His mother thought that Jesus could do something about it?

When Mary said to Jesus, **"They have no more wine,"** there must have been the implication that she expected Jesus to do something about it because of His response. Jesus said to her, **"Why involve Me? What can I do about it? My time has not yet come."** (paraphrase) That last sentence, **"My time has not yet come,"** is repeated a few times throughout the gospel of John until we come to the week of the cross when Jesus says to His disciples, **"The hour has come for the Son of Man to be glorified!"** (John 12:23)

Even though Jesus seems to resist being involved in the lack of wine details of the reception, His mother still says to the servants, **"Do whatever He tells you!"** And that's what I want you to focus on for this day: - **"Do whatever He tells you!"** Every day that we live we need to be focused on listening for His voice. I have learned that Jesus speaks to me often when I least expect it. The question is, am I ready to do whatever He tells me?

APPLICATION:

Faith is not just something you have; it is demonstrated by what you do. James writes about that in his epistle. He says in James 2:26, **"As the body without the spirit is dead, so faith without deeds is dead."** We are not only to listen for God's voice, we are to be willing to do whatever it is that He asks of us. We may not be called upon to rescue a wedding reception from failure, but we will be called upon to make a difference in the lives of those around us in some way.

VERSE TO MEMORIZE:
John 2:5

Day 15

Read – John 2:6-11

Jesus responds to the confidence His mother has in Him. He sees six large water jars sitting in the corner and says to the servants, "See those large water jars over there – fill them with water." Now, I don't know if Jesus put special emphasis on the word "fill" or not, but the Bible says **"they filled them to the brim!"** This is the same way we need to respond when Jesus asks us to do something for Him. **Ecclesiastes 9:10 says, "Whatever your hand finds to do, do it with all your might."**

Immediately after they filled the jars with water Jesus had the servants draw some out and take it to the master of the banquet. He took one taste and said, "Wow. This is great stuff!" And then he said to the bridegroom, **"Why did you wait till the end to bring out the best wine?"** (paraphrase)

APPLICATION:

There are a number of things we can learn from this passage. First of all, do not develop any preconceived ideas about what God is up to, even when it doesn't seem like He is answering your prayers. Jesus didn't give His mother any indication that He was going to do anything in response to her request. Jesus answers our prayers in three ways: "No, Yes, or Wait." In each case He knows what's best for us. We must trust Him!

The second thing I see here is the obedience of the servants: **"and they filled the water jars to the brim."** In your service to the Kingdom, always do your very best. Our Lord deserves the very best from us, always!

VERSE TO MEMORIZE:
Ecclesiastes 9:10

Day 16

John 2:13-16

"When it was almost time for the Jewish Passover,
Jesus went up to Jerusalem.
In the temple courts He found men selling
cattle, sheep and doves,
and others sitting at tables exchanging money.
So He made a whip out of
cords, and drove all from the temple area,
both sheep and cattle;
He scattered the coins of the money changers
and overturned their tables.
To those who sold doves He said,
'Get these out of here! How dare you turn
My Father's house into a market.'
His disciples remembered that it is written:
'Zeal for Your house will consume Me.'"

This passage is not so much about what Jesus does in the temple as it is about what is happening within His heart! It's all about the passion Jesus feels for this place of worship.

John records Jesus saying, **"How dare you turn My Father's house into a market."** But when Matthew writes about Jesus' cleansing of the temple, he records Jesus as saying, **"My house will be called a house of prayer, but you are making it a den of robbers."**

You see, it was not only the fact that the sacrifices needed for worship in the temple were being sold there, it was the fact that the merchants were overcharging the worshipers. They were cheating the people! Even in our day, we have seen those people who make big profits out of selling religious merchandise. God hates it when unscrupulousness marketers take advantage of others and use religion to do it.

We also need to understand that under the new covenant the divine plan of God is that He no longer resides in a structure made by human hands, but chooses to reside within our own hearts. As we embrace His grace we become His temple through the abiding Holy Spirit.

APPLICATION:

Treat fellow believers as participants in the holy temple of God! Remember that Jesus' passion for the "house of the Father" is the way He feels about His children.

VERSE TO MEMORIZE:

John 2:17

Day 17

John 2:18-20

"Then the Jews demanded of Him,
'What miraculous sign can You show us
to prove Your authority to do all this?'
Jesus answered them, 'Destroy this temple,
and I will raise it again in three days.'
The Jews replied, 'It has taken
forty-six years to build this temple,
and You are going to raise it in three days?'
But the temple He had spoken of was His body.
After He was raised from the dead,
His disciples recalled what He had said.
Then they believed the Scripture and the words
that Jesus had spoken."

When Jesus threw the money changers out of the temple, the response of the Jewish leaders was, **"What authority does He have to do something like this in our temple? And what miraculous sign can He show that will prove His**

authority?" That's when Jesus responded, **"You want to see a sign? I will show you a sign. Destroy this temple, and I will raise it again in three days."**

There were so many times when the Jews completely misunderstood what Jesus was saying. That is why it is so important for us to ask the Holy Spirit to teach us as we read and study the Scriptures! In this case the Jews were thinking, "temple, the place of worship," while Jesus was talking about His own body. Even His own disciples didn't really understand what He was saying until after the resurrection as it says here, **"After He was raised from the dead, He disciples recalled what He had said. Then they believed the Scripture and the words that Jesus had spoken."**

APPLICATION:

When we dialogue with each other we usually talk about the material world that we are a part of. We talk about our jobs, our homes, our cars, or our families. But when Jesus speaks to us He is usually sharing with us some spiritual truth. We really need to remember that! When I read the Scriptures I am seeking to know spiritual truth!

VERSE TO MEMORIZE:
I Corinthians 2:13

Day 18

John 2:23-25

"Now while He was in Jerusalem at the Passover Feast, many people saw the miraculous signs He was doing and believed in His name. But Jesus would not entrust Himself to them, for He knew all men. He did not need man's testimony about men, for He knew what was in man."

Here is a situation where people saw the things Jesus was doing and they believed in Him. However, it seems like their faith in Him was not genuine. Jesus did not respond to their faith because of His knowledge of what was in their hearts. We can say that we believe, but God knows the truth!

So what does it mean to have genuine faith? I think James actually deals with this in his epistle. He writes in James 2:14, **"What good is it, my brothers, if a man claims to have faith but has no deeds? Can such faith save him?"** Again:

faith is not just something you have, it is demonstrated by what you do!

I may say that I love God with all my heart, and that He is my all in all, but if I don't practice good stewardship, I'm really not serious. The word "stewardship" is not only about money, it is the way we use everything God has given us to use: our treasure, our talents, and our time. The way we live our lives reflects on the reality of our faith. You may say what you wish, but remember: God knows your heart!

APPLICATION:

From time to time we need to do a "faith check." Does your lifestyle reflect the depth of your faith? Remember again what James writes in chapter 2 verse 19, **"You believe that there is one God. Good! Even the demons believe that – and shudder."**

VERSE TO MEMORIZE:

James 2:14

Day 19

Read – John 3:1-8

This is one of those places in our journey with John where we need to stop and take in the view. To think that Jesus spoke about the awesome possibility of being born of the Holy Spirit, and to think He spoke these words to just one man. Nicodemus was part of the Sanhedrin, and this Jewish ruling council was very opposed to Jesus. That's one reason Nicodemus sought Jesus out after dark.

Nicodemus immediately recognized Jesus as being a wonderful teacher sent down from God above. Jesus didn't really respond to the acclamation of Nicodemus, but went right to the crux of the matter. He said to Nicodemus, **"I tell you the truth, no one can see the kingdom of God unless he is born again."** These words really threw Nicodemus. Immediately he thought of a physical birth and so he asked the obvious question, "How can anyone be physically born a second time?"

Jesus then clarified for Nicodemus exactly what He meant. He said, **"I tell you the truth, no one can enter the kingdom of God unless he is born of water and the Spirit. Flesh gives birth to flesh, but the Spirit gives birth to spirit."** I have heard this interpreted a number of ways, but I think it is very clear. In defining two births, Jesus clearly states that we must be born physically and spiritually. When He says, "born of water," it is clear to me He is referring to a physical birth. After all, what happens when the baby is ready to be born: the water breaks! Up until now the baby has been living in the water of the womb. Jesus makes it even clearer when He says, **"Flesh gives birth to flesh, but the Spirit gives birth to spirit."**

Jesus goes on to liken the Spirit to wind. We cannot see the Holy Spirit, and we cannot see wind, but as we can see the results of a strong wind, so we can see the results of the work of the Holy Spirit in the world around us.

APPLICATION:

Do we really understand what happens when we are born of the Spirit? How does being born of the Spirit affect my life? It is the Holy Spirit that enables us to be God's witness in our world. It is by God's Spirit that we are empowered to resist the temptations Satan sends our way. The fullness of the Holy Spirit is the key to living a victorious Christian life!

VERSE TO MEMORIZE:
John 3:3

Day 20

John 3:9-15

"'How can this be?' Nicodemus asked.
'You are Israel's teacher,' said Jesus,
'and do you not understand these things?
I tell you the truth, we speak of what
we know, and we testify to what we have seen,
but still people do not accept
our testimony. I have spoken to you of earthly
things and you do not believe;
how then will you believe if I speak of heavenly
things? No one has ever gone into heaven except
the One who came from heaven – the Son of Man.
Just as Moses lifted up the snake in the desert,
so the Son of Man must be lifted up,
that everyone who believes in Him
may have eternal life.'"

It seems Jesus was quite confrontational with Nicodemus. He said to him, **"You are a teacher of spiritual truth, yet you don't really understand the important truths of the**

Spirit! I have actually come from heaven and yet you do not believe My words." And then Jesus makes a prophetic statement when He says, **"Just as Moses lifted up the snake in the desert, so the Son of Man must be lifted up, that everyone who believes in Him may have eternal life."** Nicodemus doesn't really understand to what Jesus is alluding, but Jesus is pointing to the cross, which is His ultimate destiny. Always remember, the cross is the central theme in the message of the gospel.

When the apostle Paul chose to embrace the Christ whom he had persecuted, it didn't take him long to realize that the cross was central to the gospel message. He wrote in Galatians 6:14, **"May I never boast except in the cross of our Lord Jesus Christ, through which the world has been crucified to me, and I to the world."**

APPLICATION:

It is foundational to our faith to understand that what Jesus did on the cross is really what it's all about. Paul also wrote in I Corinthians 2:2, **"For I resolved to know nothing while I was with you except Jesus Christ and Him crucified."**

VERSE TO MEMORIZE:
Galatians 6:14

Day 21

Read –
John 3:16-21

Find a place to sit, because we have reached a mountain peak in the gospel of John. We need some time to take in the view! John 3:16 has been called the "golden text of the Bible." This verse has also been referred to as "the gospel in a nutshell." It is truly the essence of the gospel message!

John 3:16 give us the height and depth, the width and the length of the great love of God. The height of God's love is that it reached up into heaven and gave the very best heaven has to offer: God's only Son. The depth of God's love is that it also reached down to the depths of a sinful world and offered that world redemption. The width of God's love is the fact that it is offered to whoever believes. And the length of God's love is that it offers us eternal life. WOW!

God's love is really beyond comprehension! You may have heard people say, "How can a loving God send anyone to hell?" This is a very misunderstood question! First of all, the Bible says in II Peter 3:9, **"The Lord is not slow in keeping**

His promise, as some understand slowness. He is patient with you, not wanting anyone to perish, but everyone to come to repentance."

Hell was not created for human beings; it was created for Satan and his angels. God has done everything possible to keep us out of hell. He gave the best heaven had to offer, His only Son, and through Him offered us the gift of eternal life. He also created us with the freedom to make our own choices. If we end up in hell it will be because we chose to ignore the forgiveness God offered us, and therefore ended up under the control of Satan himself.

In this passage John makes it clear that the choice is ours to make. The choice is to believe in the Person of Jesus Christ, or to reject what He did for us. Then John tells us that it is a choice between light and darkness. And John tells us, **"men have loved darkness instead of light because their deeds are evil."**

APPLICATION:

The choices you make in life will determine where you will spend eternity. God knows your heart and He will also validate the choices you make for yourself.

VERSE TO MEMORIZE:

John 3:16

Day 22

Read –
John 3:22-30

At this time there was still a lot of attention focused on John the Baptist. It says in verse 23, **"people were constantly coming to be baptized."** John's disciples were very loyal to him, so much so that they considered this Jesus to be an intruder in John's ministry of baptism. So an argument developed between the disciples of John and a certain Jew.

So John's disciples went to John with genuine concern over what Jesus was doing. They said, **"This Jesus is also baptizing people, and everyone is going to Him."** Sounds like the same kind of jealousy that often exists between churches. But John set them straight, giving them an example from a Jewish wedding. The one who attends to the bridegroom is only interested in what the Bridegroom is interested in, and that is the Bride! When he hears the voice of the Bridegroom announcing that it is time to go and get the bride, nothing else matters.

John knew the Bride had come! He said to his disciples, **"He must increase and I must decrease."** This reminds me of the experiences I have had in doing interim pastoring where churches were between pastors. My job was not to become their pastor but to be a forerunner of the one who was to come. I tried to help them focus on the one who was to come so that the new pastor would be received with great joy! Since the time that Jesus entered the picture, John pointed his own disciples to Jesus, the Christ.

APPLICATION:

In a sense we, too, are to be forerunners of Christ, because He is coming again! And if our world does not hear of His promised return from us, they will never hear. John declared, "The Bride has arrived!" Our message is, "The Bridegroom is coming again to receive His Bride, the Church, unto Himself." What a glorious message is ours to deliver.

VERSE TO MEMORIZE:
Revelation 22:7

Day 23

John 3:31-36

"The One who comes from above is above all;
the one who is from the earth belongs to the earth,
and speaks as one from the earth.
The One who comes from heaven is above all.
He testifies to what he has seen and heard,
but no one accepts His testimony.
The man who has accepted it
has certified that God is truthful.
For the One whom God has sent
speaks the words of God,
for God gives the Spirit without limit.
The Father loves the Son and has
placed everything in His hands.
Whoever believes in the Son has eternal life,
but whoever rejects the Son will not see life,
for God's wrath remains on him."

John made it clear that the One sent from God, Jesus, has an elevated status. This elevated status comes not only from

WHO He is, but also from WHERE He has come from. Paul makes this clear from what he writes in Colossians 1:18, **"And He is the head of the body, the Church; He is the beginning and the firstborn from among the dead, so that in everything, He might have the supremacy."** And the author of Hebrews writes in Hebrews 1:4, **"So He became as much superior to the angels as the name He has inherited is superior to theirs."**

In church we say, "It's all about Him!" His name is superior to the angels' name and to ours; His knowledge is superior to ours; His power is superior to ours. He is to be our all in all! We acclaim Him Master and Lord!

The one sentence that troubles me from this passage is in verse 22 where it says, **"but no one accepts His testimony."** In the day and age when Jesus walked this earth it seems like people were responding to the works Jesus did, but had trouble with the words He spoke. Jesus did what He did to prove He was who He said He was. But it seems like the people always wanted just one more miracle. They were never satisfied.

APPLICATION:

Does Jesus Christ have an elevated status in your life? Is He not only your Savior, but your Lord? Remember, the Bible says that the day will come when **"every knee will bow and every tongue will confess that Jesus Christ is Lord."**

VERSE TO MEMORIZE:
John 3:36

ON THE TRAIL WITH JOHN THE APOSTLE

Day 24

Read – John 4:1-26

I know this is rather a lengthy passage, so let's take a couple of days to consider it. Besides, whenever one takes a lengthy hike it is necessary to pause for some nourishment. So, just as Jesus and His disciples paused here at Jacob's well for a much-needed rest and some nourishment, we are going to do the same.

The first lesson is found in the statement, **"Now He had to go through Samaria,"** (in verse 4). There were other roads one could take without going through Samaria. You see, the Jews did not like to go through Samaria because of their prejudice against the Samaritans. The Samaritans were considered to be half-breeds and not true Jews, so there was great animosity towards them. I believe when it says Jesus had to go through Samaria, it was more His submission to the leadership of the Holy Spirit.

Our lives are a combination of the choices we make along the way. Every day we make choices that determine the direction of our lives. The Bible teaches us that when we are in Christ, we have the Holy Spirit within us to help guide us in the decisions that we make. Most decisions we make on a daily basis are quite mundane, but there comes those times when we are called upon to make a difficult decision and we really don't know what to do. I believe it is in those times that God helps us to know the direction He would have us take.

On his missionary journeys the Apostle Paul tells of times when the Holy Spirit changed the direction of where he was planning to go. Even in the Christmas story, Joseph was warned in a dream to flee from Bethlehem and head for Egypt. Every time I have changed pastorates God has made it very clear to me what direction I should go.

APPLICATION:

We learn how to depend upon the guidance of the Holy Spirit by faith. And remember: God never leads us contrary to what the Bible makes clear. Also, if you are in the throes of making a decision, the direction God gives us is often not for our immediate benefit, but definitely for our ultimate benefit! Rather He guides us in the direction that will bring most glory to the Father.

VERSES TO MEMORIZE:
Proverbs 3:5-6

Day 25

Continuation of the Woman at the Well Story

It was noontime. Jesus and His disciples were weary from their journey, so they stopped at Jacob's Well near the town of Sychar. Jesus sat down by the well while the disciples went into town to buy some food. Jesus knew He had a divine appointment to keep. Before long, along came Jesus' appointment, a Samaritan woman from Sychar. It is obvious that this woman did not want to come to the well when there were other women there. She had a very poor reputation and was probably looked down upon by the other women of the town.

Now most of the time the Jews did not talk to the Samaritans. But when this woman shows up, Jesus says to her, **"Could you get Me a drink?"** She was shocked that Jesus even spoke to her. She responded, **"You are a Jew and I am a Samaritan woman. Why do You ask me for a drink?"** Then Jesus went spiritual on her; He said, **"If you knew the gift of God** and who it is that asks you for a drink, you would have asked Him and He would have given you living water." She responded, "How can I get this living water?" Jesus answered, "Everyone who drinks this water will be thirsty again, but whoever drinks the water I give him will never thirst. Indeed, the water I give him will become in him a spring of water welling up to eternal life." The woman said to Him, "Sir, give me this water so that I won't get thirsty and have to keep coming here to draw water."

One preacher I heard summarized this conversation like this: A woman came to the well to draw water. Jesus said to her, "I am in the water business Myself. The only difference is, one drink of My water and you will never be thirsty again." The woman replied, "Give me this water!"

APPLICATION:

It is so interesting how Jesus would change a discussion from the physical to the spiritual. It is actually the key to being a good witness. If only we could learn to take the normal things people talk about and turn their interest to a spiritual dimension. It is really our mandate that we tell thirsty people where they can find living water!

VERSE TO MEMORIZE:
Revelation 21:6

Day 26

Continuation of the Woman at the Well Story

Now that Jesus had this woman interested in the Living Water, He said to her, **"Go, call your husband and come back."** Now Jesus knew all about her immoral life. He was actually revealing to her the need she has for God to change her life. So she says to Him, **"I have no husband."** Then Jesus really got her attention. He said, **"You are right when you say you have no husband. The fact is, you have had five husbands, and the man you now have is not your husband."**

I'll bet we could have seen her jaw drop! He had pulled the covers back on her immoral lifestyle. She stood before Him without excuse. It's really the same feeling we have when the Holy Spirit convicts us of our sin. Her response was, **"You must be a prophet!"** And so, to get off of the subject of her immoral life, she asked him an age-old question the Samaritans had: **"Our people worship on this mountain, but you Jews** claim that the place we must worship is in Jerusalem." Jesus responded, **"The time is coming when the true worshipers will worship the Father in spirit and in truth, for they are the kind of worshipers the Father seeks."**

And then came the final revelation. The woman said, **"I know that the Christ (Messiah) is coming. When He comes, He will explain everything to us."** And Jesus said, **"I who speak to you am He!"** The dialogue has gone from water to Christ!

About this time the disciples show up. They saw Jesus talking to this Samaritan woman but they chose not to say anything about it. But at this point, the woman has been convinced, and she became a real missionary. She left her water pots behind and went back to town and tells the people, **"Come, see a man who told me everything I ever did. Could this be the Christ?"** And the townspeople followed her back to Jesus.

APPLICATION:
What can we learn from this conversation between Jesus and this Samaritan woman? Are there ways in which we can steer our conversations from the trivial to the sacred?

VERSE TO MEMORIZE:
Psalm 19:14

Day 27

Continuation of the Woman at the Well Story

While this Samaritan woman was gone, telling her story to the townspeople, the disciples break out the food they have brought back from town. They encourage Jesus to eat something, but He said to them, **"I have food to eat that you know nothing about."** These disciples are still not tuned in to the spiritual dimension of Jesus' words. They were wondering who brought Him food, when Jesus said to them, **"My food is to do the will of Him who sent Me and to finish His work."** Then Jesus painted for them a picture of the great harvest taking place in the world.

This is really God's greatest concern: the harvest field of the world. In painting the picture, Jesus made it clear that everyone has some part to play in the harvest of men's souls. He talked about the sower and the reaper; some have done the hard work, and others have reaped the benefits without the effort.

Behind this story is the reality of racism. It seems like we live our lives dealing with the labels that are put on people. Here we have the Samaritans and the Jews; the half-breeds and the "true" worshipers. In our world we hear the labels that people are forced to wear: Democrats, Republicans, Christians, Atheists, Blacks, Latinos, Asians, and more. What's interesting is that we had nothing to do with the fundamental labels that we wear; we did not choose them, they chose us. We did not choose our skin color, or where we were born, or our gender, etc. I really don't think God sees all of that. God sees us as a part of His unique creation, and He loves every one of us irrespective of the labels. I can't wait to get to heaven where none of those labels will matter.

APPLICATION:

Have you ever had an experience where it diminished any interest you had in rest or food? I especially remember one Friday evening when I came home tired and hungry, and I became involved with a person in need. The Lord answered prayer in an amazing way that night and I felt totally renewed! I hope sometime, somewhere you will experience the reality of saying, **"I have food to eat that you know nothing about."**

VERSE TO MEMORIZE:

Matthew 6:33

Day 28

John 4:39-42

"Many of the Samaritans from that town believed
in Him because of the woman's testimony,
'He told me everything I ever did.'
So when the Samaritans came to Him,
they urged Him to stay with them,
and He stayed two days.
And because of His words
many more became believers.
They said to the woman,
'We no longer believe just because
of what you said;
now we have heard for ourselves,
and we know that this man really
is the Savior of the world.'"

Have you ever tried to describe the Pacific Ocean to someone who lives in the Midwest and has never seen the ocean? Or to describe the Grand Canyon to someone who has never seen the Grand Canyon? You will never be able to adequately describe it. There is a certain awe one feels when you see either one for the first time. Likewise, you can try to describe what it's like to have a genuine relationship with Jesus Christ, but until you actually experience it, you really don't know.

There are so many names for Jesus in the New Testament that help us know Him, but it's still not the same as really knowing Him. The Samaritan woman had an encounter with Him that changed her life forever. And when she met Him at the well, the experience was so profound that she couldn't keep it to herself. She had to tell others!

The people she told believed her story, but when they met the Christ for themselves their faith deepened. I was raised in the church. I heard all of the stories about Jesus and what He did, and what He said. But when I was nine years old I had an encounter with Jesus that was very personal, and my knowledge of Him took on a new dimension. We are in the middle of our journey through John's gospel with the Apostle himself. But when you invite Jesus to walk with us on that journey, it becomes even more profound. His words are not just words, they are personal, they are profound, they are life changing.

APPLICATION:

If you haven't already, invite Jesus to walk this journey with us. Ask Him to take control of your life and to help you discover the deep truths of His word. When you do this, the journey takes on a whole new dimension, and your eyes will be opened to things you have never seen before.

VERSE TO MEMORIZE:
John 4:42

Day 29

Read – John 4:43-54

Since the underlying theme of John's gospel is believing on Jesus as the Christ, John's is extremely focused on our faith. Here in this passage Jesus is confronted by a certain political leader whose son is very ill. He begs Jesus to come and heal his son. But Jesus seems to test his integrity. He says to him, **"Unless you people see miraculous signs and wonders, you will never believe."** But this royal official is only focused on one thing: the need of his son.

Do the things we pray for suddenly become less important if the answer doesn't come just like we think it should? This royal official is really a wonderful example to us; he does not respond to what Jesus said, but insists, **"Sir, come down before my child dies."**

What Jesus said initially to him was a test of his faith, and then Jesus continued to test his faith when His final response was, **"You may go your way. Your son will live."** In other words, "I'm not coming to your home, you'll just have to trust Me. Your son has already been healed." Verse 50 says, **"The man took Jesus at His word and departed."** This royal official didn't argue with Jesus, he simply believed and did what Jesus told him to do. When he got home he found a miracle had happened, and it had happened at the very time Jesus had said to him, **"Your son will live."**

APPLICATION:

I love the simplicity of this story! We present a need to Jesus, and Jesus proceeds to test our faith. True faith responds by doing exactly what Jesus asks of us. And what does He ask of us? "That we Trust and Obey, for there is no other way to be happy in Jesus but to trust and obey."

VERSE TO MEMORIZE:

Hebrews 11:6

Day 30

Read – John 5:1-15

This is a very interesting story. In fact, biblical scholar J.P. Morgan states, "On the human level, what Jesus did that day, and what He said that day, cost Him His life. They never forgave Him."

Picture the scene – a pool surrounded by all kinds of hurting people; the blind, the crippled, and the paralyzed. Picture Jesus walking into that kind of situation. For some reason Jesus zeroes in on one particular man who was crippled. And He walks up to him and asks, **"Do you want to get well?"** You may say, that is an obvious question. But think about it for a moment. There are actually people who pray to be healed, but in reality, don't really want to be healed. Psychologists tell us there are some invalids who actually choose to be an invalid. Why is that? Because it minimizes many of the decisions they have to make in life. For them, it is a safe place to be.

This man Jesus confronted had been an invalid for thirty-eight years. But there was a belief that when the waters of this pool were stirred in some way, the first one in the water would be healed. This man responded to Jesus, **"Sir, I have no one to help me into the pool when the water is stirred. While I am trying to get in, someone else goes down ahead of me."**

Now Jesus didn't comment on the man's answer but simply said, **"Get up! Pick up your mat and walk."** As he started to respond, he was healed immediately! Now the only problem with what Jesus did was that He did it on the Sabbath. The Law said nothing is to be done on the Sabbath that even looks like work. Plus, the Jews saw this man carrying his mat, and that was also illegal on the Sabbath. Now both the man healed and Jesus were in trouble! In fact, this is where trouble for Jesus begins, and it ultimately leads to His death.

APPLICATION:

What supposed rules do we have that keep us from receiving from God His best? And do we really want what God wants for us? In considering these questions we need to be brutally honest with ourselves.

VERSE TO MEMORIZE:

Romans 8:28

Day 31

John 5:16-18

"So, because Jesus was doing these things on the Sabbath, the Jews persecuted Him. Jesus said to them, 'My Father is always at His work to this very day, and I, too, am working.' For this reason the Jews tried all the harder to kill Him; not only was He breaking the Sabbath, but He was even calling God His own Father, making Himself equal with God."

It seems that when people get a negative focus on another person, for religious reasons or for political reasons, they try to use anything that person says or does against them. This was especially true in Jesus' situation. The religious leaders of that day had come to hate Jesus. They not only hated Him, they tried to kill Him.

In this passage there are two things that disturbed the Jews: the fact that Jesus was breaking the Sabbath according to

Jewish law, and that He was making Himself equal with God by calling God His Father. They actually misunderstood why God established the Sabbath in the first place. In Ezekiel 20:12, it says, **"I gave them My Sabbaths as a sign between us, so they would know that I the Lord made them holy."** The Sabbath is a sign helping us to remember that God is holy, and any holiness we may have comes from our relationship with Him.

In the New Testament, in Mark 2:27, Jesus says, **"The Sabbath was made for man, not man for the Sabbath. So the Son of Man is Lord even of the Sabbath."** The purpose of the Sabbath is to remind us that He is Lord of all. According to the Jews, Jesus violated the Sabbath day many times. Yet, when we help others on the Sabbath, or any other day, we are honoring God!

The second complaint the Jews had was that Jesus had made Himself equal with God by calling God His Father. The only problem with that was it was true! He was God in the flesh, come to earth to set us free!

APPLICATION:

Don't allow yourself to get hung up with legalism. To verify the rightness or wrongness of anything, ask yourself some simple questions: Is it true to the Word of God? Does it honor God? Does it glorify God? Does it help others to know God?

VERSE TO MEMORIZE:
Colossians 3:17

Day 32

John 5:19-23

"Jesus gave them this answer:
'I tell you the truth, the Son can do nothing
by Himself; He can do only what He sees
His Father doing, because whatever the Father
does the Son also does. For the Father loves
the Son and shows Him all He does.
Yes, to your amazement He will show Him
even greater things than these.
For just as the Father raises the dead and gives
them life, even so the Son gives life to whom
He is pleased to give it.
Moreover, the Father judges no one,
but has entrusted all judgment to the Son,
that all may honor the Son
just as they honor the Father.
He who does not honor the Son
does not honor the Father,
who sent Him."

It says here, **"Jesus gave them this answer."** Jesus is responding to their accusation that He is calling God His Father and therefore making Himself equal with God. Jesus is validating His claim! In doing so Jesus makes three simple claims: first of all, the Son does whatever the Father gives Him to do; secondly, the Son gives life, just as the Father does.; and thirdly, all judgment has been given to the Son. Therefore, to honor the Son is to honor the Father.

The real problem is that these Jews are not interested in hearing the truth. They are stuck in their preconceived ideas. Do any of us ever get stuck in our preconceived ideas? We should always be ready to embrace the truth as God reveals it to us.

When Jesus stood before Pilate in John 18, Jesus said to him (verse 37), **"for this reason I was born, and for this I came into the world, to testify to the truth. Everyone on the side of truth listens to Me."** Jesus not only spoke the truth, He was the embodiment of truth. He said in John 14: **"I am the way and the truth and the life. No one comes to the Father except through Me."**

APPLICATION:

Be careful of your preconceived ideas. Always be a seeker of truth. Seek the truth in God's Word, and seek the truth in Jesus. He will NEVER lie to you!

VERSE TO MEMORIZE:

John 10:30

Day 33

Read –
John 5:24-30

In the previous devotion we talked about truth. Two more times in this passage Jesus says, **"I tell you the truth."** John equates hearing the truth to believing the truth. John's stated purpose for writing this gospel is that we may become believers of the truth. And John says here that if we will believe in Him we will be given eternal life. He says that we will pass from death to life.

John mentions death a couple of times in this passage. Now understand, death never means extinction of being. It literally means separation. Physical death is the separation of the soul from the body; and spiritual death is total separation from any relationship to God. In Christ, we are never separated from God. Even in physical death the Bible says, **"To be absent from the body is to be present with the Lord."** (II Corinthians 5:8)

It is also important to realize that the gift of eternal life that God has promised to all of those who believe in Christ does not begin when we die; it begins when we believe. It is quality of life and not quantity of life. Remember Jesus said, **"I have come that they may have life, and have it to the full."** (John 10:10)

APPLICATION:

Are you enjoying life to the full? That is God's plan for you. That's why He gave His life on an old rugged cross, that we might have life, an abundant life! The deeper my relationship with Jesus, the happier my life will be.

VERSE TO MEMORIZE:

John 5:24

Day 34

Read – John 5:31-40

The question asked here, and has been asked through the ages, is: *who is this Jesus?* Is He really who He says He is? The answer to that question will ultimately determine how you respond to Him. According to Jewish custom a claim is established by the word of at least two people. So Jesus reminds theses Jews that He has two witnesses to His deity, John the Baptist and the Father.

Jesus knows that these people hold John the Baptist in high regard. He mentions that John has been a light shining in the darkness, and they have accepted and enjoyed that light. But now they have made the choice to step out of that light.

Then Jesus says to them, **"I have testimony weightier than that of John."** It is not human testimony, but divine testimony. It is the very testimony of the Father, the One who actually sent Jesus to this earth. Everything Jesus does is part of the work that the Father has given Him to do.

Jesus reminds these people that in their diligent study of the scriptures and in seeking for eternal life, they have missed the goal. The truth of the matter is that these very scriptures testify to the fact that He has been sent by the Father. He is the One through whom comes eternal life.

APPLICATION:

These people think they have all they need, when in reality they have missed the boat completely. There are so many people in our world today who think in the same way. They have embraced some false teaching and are headed in the wrong direction without any awareness of their deception. The Truth is in Jesus! In fact He is "the Way, the Truth, and the Life." (John 14:6) Without Him there is no eternal life. To know eternal life is to know Jesus!

VERSE TO MEMORIZE:

John 5:39

Day 35

Read –
John 5:41-47

Jesus concludes this theme about His deity by confronting the very basis of their belief. First of all He says to them in verse 42, **"I know that you do not have the love of God in your hearts."** Jesus is challenging their basic motivation. They do not love God; and they do not love others.

Secondly, Jesus challenges them with the fact that they are so easily persuaded by the claims of others who come in their own name, and yet reject the One who has come in the name of the Father. He accuses them of soaking up the praise that comes from their peers, but have no desire for the praise that comes from God.

Jesus reminds them that He is really not their accuser: Moses is! I'll bet that got their attention! Moses was at the pinnacle of importance in their spiritual conclusions. Everything Moses ever said was true! There was no falsehood in the words of

Moses. And then Jesus reminds them in verses 46 and 47, **"If you believed Moses, you would believe Me, for he wrote about Me. But since you do not believe what he wrote, how are you going to believe what I say?"**

APPLICATION:

From time to time we all need to take inventory on the foundation of our belief system. What do I really believe? And where do those beliefs come from? What is the level of truth that I am willing to die for? Once again it comes back to Jesus: He should be the foundation for my belief system! That's why I believe it is so important for us to have a biblical world view. It's the only view that really answers all my questions. Take a moment and analyze your own belief system.

VERSES TO MEMORIZE:

Romans 10:9-10

Day 36

Read – John 6:1-15

This is a most fascinating story! We could say this is a good place to stop on the trail and take in the vista before us. It was the very first passage I ever preached from. I was reading the story when two phrases jumped out at me. The first one is when Andrew tells Jesus that there is a boy with a small lunch: five loaves and two fish. And then Andrew says, **"What are they among so many?"** (verse 9, KJV) And the second phrase is in verse 11 **"And Jesus took the loaves."** (KJV)

Jesus has called on us all to share our witness with our world. However, there is so much need; so many who do not know about the grace of God; so much evil in the world – what am I among so many? What can I do that will really make a difference? The answer comes not in my abilities or resources but in my ability to let God use me as He will. Yes, what am I among so many? But then, I allowed Jesus to take the loaves, to take my unworthiness and use it for His glory!

This is not only a powerful story, it is also a wonderful illustration of the power of God to accomplish His purpose. The disciples were totally unprepared to respond to the need of this great crowd of people. But Jesus wasn't caught unprepared! When Jesus said to Philip, **"Where shall we buy bread for these people to eat?"** The Bible says He asked Philip the question to test him. Did you know that God places His tests in our path quite regularly? But remember, when God tests us He is not interested in any resources we might have, He is interested in seeing just how strong our faith is in His ability.

This miracle was really not done for the people who were fed, it was done for the disciples who later would become the very foundation of His Church.

APPLICATION:

In living your life, on what do you focus? Do you focus on what you have, or do you focus on what He has? He is our resource! Without Him, we can do nothing! When God calls you to do something for Him, don't look at your lack of ability, rather look at His ability and your willingness to let Him do it through you.

VERSE TO MEMORIZE:
Romans 12:2

Day 37

John 6:16-21

"When evening came, His disciples went down to the lake, where they got into a boat and set off across the lake for Capernaum. By now it was dark, and Jesus had not yet joined them.
A strong wind was blowing and the waters grew rough. When they had rowed three or three and a half miles, they saw Jesus approaching the boat, walking on the water; and they were terrified.
But He said to them, 'It is I; don't be afraid.'
Then they were willing to take Him into the boat, and immediately the boat reached the shore where they were heading."

John keeps the details of this story to a minimum. Luke gives us a little more detail as he tells the story in Luke 6. We learn from Luke that Jesus instructed His disciples to go ahead of Him across the lake. According to Luke, Jesus came to the disciples in the fourth watch of the night, which is about 3:00 AM. Now, John also doesn't tell us about Peter walking on the water, but Matthew does in his account in Matthew 14.

But in essence this story is really a continuation of the test that began with the feeding of the five thousand. Have you ever wondered what happened to the leftovers that were collected after the miracle of feeding the five thousand? Think about it, there were twelve baskets of leftovers collected, and there were twelve disciples that collected them. Now the boy with the lunch certainly did not try to take all of those leftovers home. Some Bible scholars think each disciple had the leftovers from one of the baskets. So picture the scene.: twelve disciples, who had just witnessed an amazing miracle, each one holding a bag of leftovers, sitting in a boat in the middle of a storm, in the middle of the night, without the presence of Jesus. How is your faith?

The only one who seems to excel during this test is Peter. Seeing this figure walking on the water, Peter says, **"Lord, if it's You, tell me to come to You on the water."** (Matthew 14:28) In essence, Peter is saying, "Lord, I'll show You my faith!" Little did he know that he was biting off more than he could chew. His attempt at faith ended in failure.

APPLICATION:

When God answers a prayer of ours in some miraculous way, have you found that your faith is often tested in some way following such an answer? God has a way of keeping us humble in the midst of our circumstances. The Bible says, **"So, if you think you are standing firm, be careful that you don't fall."** (I Corinthians 10:12)

VERSES TO MEMORIZE:
I Corinthians 2:4-5

Day 38

John 6:22-24

"The next day the crowd that had stayed on the
opposite shore of the lake
realized that only one boat had been there, and
that Jesus had not entered
it with His disciples, but that they had gone away
alone. Then some boats
from Tiberias landed near the place where the
people had eaten the bread
after the Lord had given thanks. Once the crowd
realized that neither Jesus
nor His disciples were there, they got into the
boats and went to Capernaum
in search of Jesus."

The next day the people who had been fed were asking where Jesus had gone. The feeding event ended with the people attempting to make Jesus some kind of king. But all at once, He was gone! Where did He go? I would entitle this section, "In Search of Jesus!" They knew of only one boat that had been docked on the shore, and the disciples had taken off in that boat, and they knew Jesus wasn't with them. Where has He gone?

While the people were wondering just where Jesus had gone, some boats arrived from Tiberias. Many of the people boarded these boats in order to go to the other side of the lake. We know the people were really puzzled by Jesus' disappearance because when they arrived at the other side of the lake, where they found Him, they said to Him, in verse 25, **"Rabbi, when did You get here?"**

I think it's good when people are searching for Jesus! More people ought to be searching for Jesus. However, the question that may be asked is, why are you looking for Jesus? What do you want to receive when you find Him? What do you want Him to do for you?

APPLICATION:

If you find that you also have been searching for Jesus, there is a promise in the Bible that is just for you. Jeremiah 29:13 says, **"You will seek Me and find Me when you seek Me with all your heart."**

VERSE TO MEMORIZE:

Jeremiah 29:13

Day 39

John 6:25-29

"When they found Him on the other side of the lake, they asked Him, 'Rabbi, when did You get here?' Jesus answered, 'I tell you the truth, you are looking for Me, not because you saw the miraculous signs but because you ate the loaves and had your fill. Do not work for food that spoils, but for food that endures to eternal life, which the Son of Man will give you. On Him God the Father has placed His seal of approval.' Then they asked Him, 'What must we do to do the works God requires?' Jesus answered, 'The work of God is this: to believe in the One He has sent.'"

We know from scripture that Jesus knows all about us. We cannot fool Him. He knows what makes us tick. So when they found Jesus on the other side of the lake, and they asked Him, **"When did You get here?"** He immediately revealed their inner motives in looking for Him. He says, **"You're not looking for Me because of My miracles, you're only** looking for Me because you were fed. But since we're talking about food, let Me tell you, desire good spiritual food that will bring you eternal life." (paraphrase)

Their next question was, **"What must we do to do what God requires?" And Jesus says, "Believe in Me, the One whom God the Father has sent."** (paraphrase) Do you remember what we shared earlier about why John wrote his gospel? He tells us in John 20:31, **"I have written so you may believe that Jesus is the Christ, the Son of God, and that by believing you may have life in His name."**

APPLICATION:

The bottom line in the gospel of John is that we might believe in Jesus the Christ, and in believing comes the gift of eternal life. The other thing that is very clear here is when we say we believe, God knows the truth. Remember, God knows whether your faith is genuine or not! I Samuel 16:7 says, **"Man looks at the outward appearance, but the Lord looks at the heart."**

VERSE TO MEMORIZE:
I Samuel 16:7

Day 40

Read – John 6:30-59

This is a long passage, but it is difficult to break it up because it's all tied together. This is also where the trail through the gospel of John gets a little rough. In order for any of us to really understand this part of our journey we need to rely on the Holy Spirit to teach us God's truth. Are you ready?

Jesus has just challenged the people to desire good spiritual food. Their response is to bring up the manna that Moses fed the Israelites in the desert. It's almost like they are saying, **"You gave us some loaves and fish, but Moses gave our people bread from heaven every single day. It was a real miracle!"** Jesus challenges them in verses 32-33, **"Jesus said to them, 'I tell you the truth, it is not Moses who has given you the bread from heaven, but it is My Father who gives you the true bread from heaven. For the bread of God is He who comes down from heaven and gives life to the world."**

Their response was, **"Give us this bread!"** And Jesus responded, **"I am the bread of life. He who comes to Me will never go hungry, and he who believes in Me will never be thirsty."** When they heard Jesus say that He was "the bread of life," they didn't hear anything else. That was just too much! In essence, they went on to say, "We know His mother and His father. He's a man just like us. How could He come down from heaven?"

Jesus takes it a step further when He says in verse 51, **"I am the living bread that came down from heaven. If anyone eats of this bread, he will live forever. This bread is My flesh, which I will give for the life of the world."** It almost sounds cannibalistic. At least that's what they thought, because their response was, **"How can this man give us His flesh to eat?"** But then it gets worse; Jesus invites them to drink His blood. Verse 53: **"Jesus said to them, 'I tell you the truth, unless you eat the flesh of the Son of Man and drink His blood, you have no life in you.'"**

APPLICATION:

It is impossible for us to go into the depths of this passage, but to put it simply, what happens when we eat and drink anything? It becomes a part of us and it gives us physical life. You've heard the phrase, "You are what you eat!" Jesus yielded His body and His blood so that we may partake of His sacrifice which results in spiritual life. In Exodus, on the night the Israelites left Egypt, they ate the sacrificial lamb and spread its blood over the doorposts, and it brought them deliverance. Communion is the sacrament that symbolizes this for us.

VERSE TO MEMORIZE:
John 6:35

Day 41

Read – John 6:60-71

After Jesus' words about "eating His flesh and drinking His blood" we learn that many of His disciples **"turned back and no longer followed Him"** (verse 66). Even His own disciples were puzzled by His words, and they began to grumble among themselves. Verse 60 says, **"His disciples said, 'This is a hard teaching. Who can accept it?'"** Jesus then asked them, **"Does this offend you?"** (verse 61) And then Jesus explains to them that His teaching was spiritual not literal. He says in verse 63, **"The Spirit gives life; the flesh counts for nothing. The words I have spoken to you are spirit and they are life."**

Then Jesus asks His disciples the big question, **"You do not want to leave too, do you?"** (verse 67) And of course it is Peter who immediately responds with, **"Lord, to whom shall we go? You have the words of eternal life. We believe and know that You are the Holy One of God"** (verses 68-

69). Jesus' response to Peter's declaration of faith is quite interesting; He lets them know that there is one of them who has not believed. In verse 71 John identifies him for us – Judas!

APPLICATION:

When we become true believers, it doesn't mean that we understand everything we read in God's Word. That's why we are admonished to live by faith! As we grow in the faith the Holy Spirit enlightens us day by day. Like the old hymn says, "we will understand it better by and by." How do you handle those things that you don't fully understand? In this passage, several followers of Jesus chose to throw in the towel and walk away. Personally, I choose to stand with Peter - **"Lord, where shall we go? You have the words of eternal life!"**

VERSE TO MEMORIZE:
Romans 1:16

Day 42

Read – John 7:1-13

The tide of public opinion was changing. Some of those who had followed Jesus were now seeking to take His life. This passage tells us that the Feast of Tabernacles was approaching. In the past Jesus and His disciples had been very faithful in their attendance at the Jewish Feast celebrations. But this time Jesus is no hurry to go to Jerusalem. Was He afraid? No, He wasn't. It wasn't a matter of fear, but of timing. He said once again to His disciples, **"The right time for Me has not yet come."** (verse 6)

Some of Jesus' own brothers pressured Him to go to the Feast. They argued that no one who really wants to develop a following is going to hide himself. But Jesus was marching to the beat of a different drummer. He was seeking to fulfill the Father's will for His life. What God personally calls us to do doesn't always make sense to others.

After the discussion had subsided, Jesus' disciples went on up to the Feast, leaving Jesus behind. Shortly thereafter Jesus also went up to the Feast, but He went secretly. Now the Jewish religious leaders had actually been looking for Him. After all, they wanted to kill Him. And so, they were asking, **"Where is that man?"** (verse 11). This passage ends with a summary of the debate that was taking place. Verse 12 says, **"Among the crowds there was widespread whispering about Him. Some said, 'He is a good man.' Others replied, 'No, He deceives the people.'"**

APPLICATION:

Jesus is clear here when He says, **"My time has not yet come."** Timing is crucial! I think of the words of Isaiah in Isaiah 55:8, **"For My thoughts are not your thoughts, neither are your ways My ways declares the Lord."** God's plan is perfect! God's timing is perfect! And yet, we seem to persist in our own planning. God is so patient and we are so impatient! If you find yourself in a crisis, relax, place it all in God's hands and obediently submit to His divine will. It will make all the difference in the world.

VERSE TO MEMORIZE:
Isaiah 55:8

Day 43

Read – John 7:14-24

We learn here that Jesus didn't go public at the Feast of Tabernacles until halfway through the Feast. Then He went to the temple courts and began to teach. His teaching was such that the people were amazed at His wisdom. Jesus tells the people that His teaching is actually from God; it is not His own teaching. Then He exposes their hypocrisy. He says to them, **"Has not Moses given you the law? Yet not one of you keeps the law. Why are you trying to kill Me?"** (verse 19)

That question had to cut to the heart! Jesus exposed their evil motives, yet they were not ready to plead guilty. They refused His accusation. They replied, **"Who is trying to kill You?"** (verse 20) Folks, it does no good to deny the truth when God convicts us of our sin. After all, He knows us better than we know ourselves! He cannot deal with our sin until we confess our sin. The word *confess* actually means "to say the same thing." In other words, when I confess my sin to God I am saying the same thing as God says about my sin. And until we agree with God regarding our sin, we have no hope!

Jesus goes on to give them an example of their hypocrisy. They are willing to circumcise a child on the Sabbath Day, and yet are unwilling to recognize God's divine healing on the Sabbath. Jesus says to them, **"Stop judging by mere appearances, and make a right judgment."** (verse 24)

APPLICATION:

I can remember chairing some church board meetings when we needed to hear these words of Jesus: **"Stop judging by mere appearances, and make a right judgment."** How quick we are to judge in some situations. It would behoove us to slow down and seek God's will before making our own judgments. The granting of wisdom is one prayer request that God has promised us He will answer. James 1:5, **"If any of you lacks wisdom, he should ask God, who gives generously to all without finding fault, and it will be given to him."**

VERSE TO MEMORIZE:
James 1:5

Day 44

John 7:25-29

"At that point some of the people of Jerusalem began to ask, 'Isn't this the man they are trying to kill? Here He is, speaking publicly, and they are not saying a word to Him. Have the authorities really concluded that He is the Christ? But we know where this man is from; when the Christ comes, no one will know where He is from.' Then Jesus, still teaching in the temple courts, cried out, 'Yes, you know Me, and you know where I am from. I am not here on My own, but He who sent Me is true. You do not know Him, but I know Him because I am from Him and He sent Me.'"

On the one hand the people are amazed at Jesus' teaching. Even the Jewish religious leaders are impressed. But on the other hand, in their sight, He is just another man. After all, they know where He comes from. They know who His father and mother are. So how can He be the Christ when He is just another man?

It is quite natural for human beings to pass judgment on all that we see and hear. We are very earthy individuals! But as we study scripture we see that through the ages God has used mere man to fulfill His great plan, over and over again. He started with Abraham, then there were many others: Noah, Elijah, Elisha, Moses, Joshua, David, and the list goes on. One time God even used a talking donkey. You can read about it in Numbers 22:21-31. If He can use a donkey, then I'm sure He can use you or me.

Jesus goes on to agree with these people that they do know who He is. But then He says to them, **"You don't really know Me, and you don't really know where I am from. I am from the Father, and you don't really know Him!"** (paraphrase)

APPLICATION:

We need to remember that we not only live in a physical dimension, we also live in a spiritual dimension. The spirit world is all around us. And as long as we are on this side of glory our understanding of the spiritual world will be limited. The wonderful truth is, as we live on this earthly plain, Jesus promised us that the Holy Spirit would actually guide us into all truth. We need to allow Him to be our divine Teacher.

VERSE TO MEMORIZE:
John 14:26

Day 45

Read –
John 7:30-36

This passage starts out in verse 30 with these words, **"At this they tried to seize Him, but no one laid a hand on Him, because His time had not yet come."** We have already read several times that **"His time had not yet come."** This is John's way of pointing us toward the cross. It's almost like having a series of signs along our trail through John's gospel saying, "We're not there yet!" Even though John does not use the word *cross*, he points to the reality of the cross over and over again.

This passage gives us a clear picture of the people's response to Jesus. Verse 31 says, **"Many in the crowd put their faith in Him."** But others, who were actually on the side of religion, sought to kill Him. Verse 32b tells us, **"Then the chief priests and the Pharisees sent temple guards to arrest Him."** It's a divided response! The same is true today. Many put their faith in Him, and then there are others who refuse to give Him the time of day.

In verse 33 Jesus says something that confuses all of them. He tells them that He is not going to be around for long. He has plans to go away. And when they look for Him, He will not be found. And where He is going, they cannot come. So many times throughout the gospel of John Jesus speaks in spiritual terms, while His hearers are thinking in earthly terms. But when He says that He will be leaving them, they interpret it to mean that He is going to the Greeks in order to teach them.

APPLICATION:

In over 50 years in pastoral ministry I have discovered that when we are faced with a dilemma of some kind, we tend to figure out in our own minds how it will work out. The trouble is, usually it doesn't go that way. God is very creative in the answers He sends our way. He has surprised me more often than not. And that's really what faith is all about. We need to learn how to trust Him; how to put our problems in His hands and leave them there. It may seem that He is slow in His response, but I have found that He is always on time!

VERSE TO MEMORIZE:
Psalm 9:10

Day 46

Read – John 7:37-44

A key phrase in this passage is in verse 37: **"On the last and greatest day of the Feast, Jesus stood and said in a loud voice, 'If anyone is thirsty, let him come to Me and drink. Whoever believes in Me, as the Scripture has said, streams of living water will flow from within him.'"**

The Feast of Tabernacles was one of the most important Feasts on the Jewish calendar. It lasted for eight days and commemorated God's miraculous provision for the Israelites during their wilderness wandering. Every day of this Feast the priests would gather water from the Pool of Siloam and carry it up the Temple steps and pour it out, where pipes would carry it to the altar. As the priests carried the water, the people would sing and shout praises to the Lord. The Talmud (portion of Jewish rabbinic teaching) says, "He who has not seen the rejoicing at the place of the water-drawing has never seen rejoicing in his life."

Imagine the scene. On the last and most celebrative day of the Feast of Tabernacles with the priests pouring out water from the Pool of Siloam, and the people rejoicing with great enthusiasm, Jesus stands up and says in a loud voice, in essence, "I am the water of life! If anyone is thirsty, let him come to Me." Again Jesus was speaking in spiritual terms. And John makes it clear here that Jesus was speaking about the Holy Spirit, who would indwell everyone who believes in the Christ.

Here at the climax of this great celebration Jesus was telling them the solution to their spiritual drought is to be found in Him, the true water of life. What a declaration! Once again, the people are divided in their response to His words. Some believed and others sought to seize Him because they thought He was spouting blasphemy.

APPLICATION:

C.S. Lewis made the statement, "Jesus is either a liar, Lord, or a lunatic!" He claimed to be Lord. He claimed to be God. Do I believe Him, and do I believe Him with all my heart? There is no middle ground. You and I are either on one side or the other. Eternal life depends on the choice you make.

VERSES TO MEMORIZE:
John 4:13-14

Day 47

Read – John 7:45-52

When the temple guards (who were sent out to arrest Jesus) came back without their man, they were asked, **"Why didn't you bring Him in?"** Their answer is classic - **"Because no one ever spoke the way this man does!"** And the Pharisees responded, **"You mean He has deceived you also?"**

Nicodemus, who was a Pharisee, and also the one who had come to Jesus at night because of his interest in what Jesus was teaching, spoke up for Jesus. He said to the other Pharisees, **"Does our law condemn anyone without first hearing him to find out what he is doing?"**

Do you remember what Peter said to Jesus in John 6:68, **"Lord, You have the words of eternal life!"** Someone once told me that if I really wanted to grow as a Christian I needed to find something in the Bible that Jesus said, and do it! Never minimize anything that Jesus said. That's why I like a red letter edition Bible, because the words of Jesus stand out.

APPLICATION:

Develop a real affinity for the words of Jesus. Study His words. Ask the Holy Spirit to be your divine Teacher as you seek to apply those things Jesus said. When you read something Jesus said, ask yourself, how does this apply to me?

VERSES TO MEMORIZE:

Psalm 119:9, 11

Day 48

Read –
John 8:1-11

The Pharisees were always focused on the letter of the law. They were always looking for someone who was breaking the law, and when it came to Jesus, they felt that if they could expose Him relative to His handling of the law, they could bring Him down. In this passage the Pharisees bring a woman to Jesus who was caught in the very act of adultery. The law of Moses said she should be stoned; what would Jesus say?

The timing is perfect. Jesus is teaching a crowd of people and they are very interested in this seeming dilemma. How would Jesus respond? The interesting thing about this story is the fact that Jesus said nothing in response to their accusations. It wasn't in what He said, but in what He did. He stooped down and began to write in the dust of the ground. The question through the ages has always been, what did He write? Some scholars believe that Jesus began to list one by one the sins of the accusers. Finally Jesus stood up and said,

"If any of you is without sin, let him be the first to throw a stone at her."

When these Pharisees saw what Jesus wrote, and what He said, one by one they began to walk away. When they were all gone, Jesus said to the woman, **"Woman, where are they? Has no one condemned you? . . . "Then neither do I condemn you. Go now and leave your life of sin."**

While Jesus was on this earth it seems He had little patience with hypocrites. But to those who were willing to admit their sin, He showed great mercy. The Bible says in Psalm 86:5, **"You are forgiving and good, O Lord, abounding in love to all who call to You."**

APPLICATION:

Don't ever take God's mercy for granted. He is still a holy God and He detests sin in our lives. But if we are willing to confess our sin and repent or turn from it, His mercy and grace is always available.

VERSE TO MEMORIZE:
Psalm 86:5

Day 49

Read – John 8:12-20

In John's gospel we have what is known as the seven great "*I Am*" sayings of Jesus. They are:
- "I Am the Bread of life." (John 6:35)
- "I Am the Light of the world." (John 8:12)
- "I Am the Door." (John 10:9)
- "I Am the good Shepherd." (John 10:11)
- "I Am the Resurrection and the Life." (John 11:25-26)
- "I Am the Way, the Truth, and the Life." (John 14:6)
- "I Am the true Vine." (John 15:1-5)

We were introduced to the first of these sayings in John chapter 6 right after Jesus had fed the 5,000. The people were ecstatic about being fed with the loaves and fish. But Jesus says to them in verse 35, **"I Am the Bread of life. He who comes to Me will never go hungry, and he who believes in Me will never be thirsty."**

In the scripture we are looking at today we hear the second of these sayings. In verse 12 Jesus says, **"I Am the Light of the world. Whoever follows Me will never walk in darkness, but will have the light of life."** It seems to me that in these sayings Jesus is telling us, "Whatever it is that you really need, I Am It! Here in the eighth chapter, when Jesus says, **"I Am the Light of the world,"** the Pharisees challenged His testimony. According to Jewish law, for any testimony to be true, it must be substantiated by two witnesses. And Jesus response was, **"I am One who testifies for Myself; my other witness is the Father, who sent Me."** (verse 18)

Verse 19 says, **"Then they asked Him, 'Where is Your Father?' 'You do not know Me or My Father,' Jesus replied. 'If you knew Me, you would know My Father also.'"** This passage ends with, **"Yet no one seized Him, because His time had not yet come."**

APPLICATION:

There is that statement again, "His time had not yet come." Once again John is looking down the road towards the cross. The very reason Jesus came to our world was to give His life for our sin on the cross. The cross is the pinnacle of the gospel story. To identify with Jesus is to identify with His cross.

VERSE TO MEMORIZE:
I Corinthians 2:2

Day 50

Read – John 8:21-30

I may be weird, but I see some real humor here. The Pharisees were really perplexed by the words of Jesus. They kept trying to interpret what He was saying so they might understand it. But Jesus is speaking in spiritual terms. This time when Jesus said, **"I am going away, and you will look for Me, and you will die in your sins. Where I go, you cannot come."** (verse 21) They interpreted these words to mean that Jesus was going to kill Himself.

Once again, in this passage, John points to the cross. In verse 28 Jesus says, **"When you have lifted up the Son of Man, then you will know that I am the One I claim to be and that I do nothing on my own but speak just what the Father has taught Me."** And even though the people really did not understand all that Jesus was saying, including His own disciples, this passage ends with the words, **"Even as He spoke, many put their faith in Him."**

APPLICATION:

Have you ever had trouble understanding the words of Jesus? I know I have from time to time. That's why we need the Holy Spirit to be our divine Teacher. Also, when God reveals His divine truth to us, it is only as we find ourselves in a spirit of acceptance that we begin to understand what He is saying. The more I reach out to embrace His truth, the more of His truth He reveals to me. If you read the Word of God with a spirit of denial, then you will find yourself condemned just as these Pharisees were when Jesus said to them, **"You will die in your sins."**

VERSE TO MEMORIZE:

John 8:12

Day 51

Read – John 8:31-41

Many people believe that God's grace is automatic from the point where we choose to believe. But here in verse 31 Jesus talks about a conditional salvation. He says, **"If you hold to My teaching, you are really My disciples. Then you will know the truth, and the truth will set you free."** What happens if we don't hold to His teaching? To me, this is the motivation to keep our relationship with the Lord fresh and up to date. I have known some people who failed to hold on to the teachings of Jesus, and it really didn't end well for them.

In this passage Jesus confronts the Pharisees relative to this "Father issue." They have challenged Him relative to the claims He has made about His Father; and now He challenges them. He accuses them of being slaves to sin. But they argue, **"we are not slaves, but children of Abraham."** Jesus informs them that He has come to set them free even though they don't see the need to be set free. It seems like they did or did not understand what Jesus was saying when they respond in verse 41, **"We are not illegitimate children – The only Father we have is God Himself."**

APPLICATION:

Make sure you know what family you are in! In verse 44 Jesus says to them, **"You belong to your father the devil . . . "** In reality we were born into the wrong family. But Jesus came and provided the way for us to be adopted into the Family of God. Paul writes in Romans 8:16, **"The Spirit Himself testifies with our spirit that we are God's children."**

VERSES TO MEMORIZE:

Galatians 4:6-7

Day 52

Read –
John 8:42-47

This is a profound passage in John's gospel. In these six verses Jesus brings it all home. In verse 42 Jesus says, **"If God were your Father, you would love Me, for I came from God and now am here."** Think about that for a moment: **"If God were your Father, you would love Me!"** This is the essence of our relationship with God – LOVE!

Jesus goes on to explain why these Pharisees are unable to understand what He has been saying. I think verse 44 is the most powerful verse in this whole chapter: **"You belong to your father, the devil, and you want to carry out your Father's desire. He was a murderer from the beginning, not holding to the truth, for there is no truth in him. When he lies, he speaks his native language, for he is a liar and the father of lies."**

I love that phrase that says, **"When he lies, he speaks his native language."** We live in a world today that glorifies falsehood. Educators don't tell us the truth; politicians don't tell us the truth; the media doesn't tell us the truth, and the commercials on television are not truthful. Sometimes I think we hear so much untruth that we may not recognize the truth when we hear it.

Jesus really defines truth for us. When He appeared before Pilate in John chapter 18, Jesus said to Pilate, **"In fact, for this reason I was born, and for this I came into the world, to testify to the truth. Everyone on the side of truth listens to Me."**

APPLICATION:

As followers of Jesus Christ we need to be lovers of truth! If we are not careful we will let the mood of the day desensitize us to the falsehood that surrounds us. We see so much hatred in our world today. I believe hatred and falsehood are in a real close relationship with each other. In the 6th chapter of Ephesians Paul talks to us about the armor of God. And the very first piece of that armor that Paul mentions is truth. He says, **"Stand firm then, with the belt of truth buckled around your waist . . ."** (Ephesians 6:14)

VERSE TO MEMORIZE:
III John 4

Day 53

Read – John 8:48-59

It seems like the animosity against Jesus just continued to grow. The Pharisees could not accept the fact that Jesus was much more than just a man. Now their accusations turn into name-calling. They call Him a demon-possessed Samaritan. That is the worst thing they can think of. Jesus has done nothing close to deserving that kind of title. I have noticed that when people disagree with each other, in order to make their case they usually overstate the facts. In this section, Jesus actually calls them "liars." Jesus mentions Abraham once again in this section. He tells them that before Abraham ever existed, He was! They had no way to digest that statement. It just made them angrier.

Politically speaking, we have seen much hatred in our present day and age. And that hatred has progressed to such a degree that it has caused people to resort to violence. And that violence has resulted in the loss of life. That is almost what happens here. These Pharisees become so incensed they pick up stones to stone Jesus. But somehow, He is able to slip away from them.

APPLICATION:

Hatred is not always a bad thing. There are some things we should hate. Things like the evil acts people do to each other. Cheating, lying, greed: these are all things to hate. Jesus hated those kinds of things. In Proverbs 6:16-19 it says, **"There are six things the Lord hates, seven that are detestable to Him: haughty eyes, a lying tongue, hands that shed innocent blood, a heart that devises wicked schemes, feet that are quick to rush into evil, a false witness that pours out lies and a man who stirs up dissension among brothers."** But at the same time, our hatred needs to be a controlled hatred. Hatred out of control is never good.

VERSES TO MEMORIZE:

Titus 3:5a

Day 54

*Read –
John 9:1-12*

It's interesting to me that the scriptural stories of Jesus' healing miracles are all unique. It seems they are tailor-made to the individual. In this story, there is no dialogue between Jesus and the blind man He healed. It seems more like a teaching moment for His disciples, and ultimately for us! And Jesus didn't just touch the man; rather, He made some mud and placed it on the man's eyes. And that still didn't result in his healing. Jesus told him to go and wash in the Pool of Siloam. As the man obeyed what Jesus told him to do, he was healed.

Apply the facts of this story to how God heals people today. God is always the initiator of our healing. Our obedience to His Word is one of the keys to our healing. Like Mary said to the servants in Jesus' first miracle in Cana of Galilee, **"whatever He says to you, do it!"**

Now, the teaching moment with the disciples that takes place with this miracle is in the question they asked, **"Rabbi, who sinned, this man or his parents, that he was born blind?"** (verse 2) People seem to believe that whatever goes wrong in our lives must have some reason. We think we must have done something that angered God. Our God is not like that at all! He is a merciful and gracious God. He is often hurt by our disobedience, but He is not a vengeful God. There are negative things that happen in our lives over which we have no control. In those situations He wants to be a part of the solution. He is there to help us, to minister to our every need, and to bring healing as He sees fit.

There is a great deal of human nature in this story. The man healed doesn't have any idea of who Jesus is. And his healing seemed to change even what he looked like. You see, he had no idea of what it was like to see. He had been born blind. The look on his face must have been awesome. I believe when we choose to receive God's wonderful gift of salvation, we look different also!

APPLICATION:

Don't ever put God in a box. Don't develop preconceived ideas on how you think God will respond to your need. He may choose to use your need for His glory, or your ultimate healing may wait until you are ushered into glory. Learn to trust Him and obey Him, and leave all results in His hands.

VERSE TO MEMORIZE:
III John 2

Day 55

Read – John 9:13-34

This is a most interesting dialogue between the blind man who was healed, his neighbors, his parents and the Pharisees. We must stop along the trail to listen to this. First of all, this man was born blind which makes this miracle exceptional. It has never been done before! After hearing his story, his neighbors bring him to the Pharisees, who question him mercilessly. They ask the same questions over and over - **"How was your sight restored? - Who did it? - What do you have to say about this man who did it?"**

After the questioning became repetitious, the man healed got a little sarcastic. He says to them in verse 27, **"I have told you already and you did not listen. Why do you want to hear it again? Do you want to become His disciples, too?"** And then, in verses 30-33 he gives them a mini sermon. He says to the Pharisees who claim they don't even know where Jesus came from, **"Now that is remarkable! You don't know where He comes from, yet He opened my eyes. We know that God does not listen to sinners. He listens to the godly man who does His will. Nobody has ever heard of opening the eyes of a man born blind. If this man were not from God, He could do nothing."**

This man's parents were also questioned. But in fear of the Jews they refused to commit themselves. Their response was, **"He is of age; ask him."** (verse 23) So here we have a great dilemma. A great miracle is performed by Jesus, but it was performed on the Sabbath, which was against the law. So, how can a man who claims He comes from God break God's law? Jesus even asked the question in Mark 3:4, **"Then Jesus asked them, 'Which is lawful on the Sabbath: to do good or to do evil, to save life or to kill?'"**

APPLICATION:

This dilemma really comes down to the very purpose of the law. The law was given to help men do the right thing. It was not given arbitrarily to make our life miserable. The law is a good thing when it operates within the right context. The question should be, "What will ultimately help us and bring glory to God?" I am continually amazed at the simplicity that is at the heart of our relationship with God.

VERSES TO MEMORIZE:
Psalm 145:9 and I Timothy 1:8

Day 56

John 9:35-41

"Jesus heard that they had thrown him out, and when He found him, He said, 'Do you believe in the Son of Man?' 'Who is he, sir?' the man asked. 'Tell me so that I may believe in Him.' Jesus said, 'You have now seen Him; in fact, He is the one speaking with you.' Then the man said, 'Lord, I believe,' and he worshiped Him. Jesus said, 'For judgment I have come into this world, so that the blind will see and those who see will become blind.' Some Pharisees who were with him heard him say this and asked, 'What? Are we blind too?' Jesus said, 'If you were blind, you would not be guilty of sin; but now that you claim you can see, your guilt remains.'"

Jesus uses this miracle to speak about spiritual blindness. What do you think? Which is worse, physical blindness or spiritual blindness? There are many people in our world who are blessed with physical vision, but who lack the spiritual vision Jesus is talking about here.

So how do we develop spiritual vision? It begins with the words the formerly blind man said in verse 38, **"Lord, I believe."** That is the very essence of John's gospel, that we might believe. And when we truly believe, Jesus gives us the Holy Spirit, who takes up residence within us, and who gives us spiritual vision.

APPLICATION:

Have you developed, by the power of the Holy Spirit, spiritual vision? Now I believe two things about spiritual vision. First of all, it is something that grows within us just as our relationship with the Lord grows. Secondly, it does not reach completeness until we are united in Christ in glory. Remember Paul's words in I Corinthians 13:12, **"Now we see but a poor reflection as in a mirror; then we shall see face to face. Now I know in part; then I shall know fully, even as I am fully known."**

VERSE TO MEMORIZE:
I Corinthians 13:12

Day 57

John 10:1-5

"I tell you the truth, the man who does not enter the sheep pen by the gate, but climbs in by some other way, is a thief and a robber. The man who enters by the gate is the shepherd of his sheep. The watchman opens the gate for him, and the sheep listen to his voice. He calls his own sheep by name and leads them out. When he has brought out all his own, he goes on ahead of them, and his sheep follow him because they know his voice. But they will never follow a stranger; in fact, they will run away from him because they do not recognize a stranger's voice."

Baaa! Chapter 10 of John's gospel is all about the Shepherd and His flock. I say *Baaa* because I'm one of His flock: are you? I can just picture us rounding a corner of the trail and seeing before us beautiful pastures, full of peaceful, grazing sheep. As we listen, Jesus begins to talk to us about the special relationship we share as sheep with their Shepherd.

Now sheep have been referred to as dumb animals. I don't know about you, but I plead guilty! But there are some wonderful things we learn about sheep in Jesus' words. First of all, He protects His sheep. He is aware when a thief or robber, or even a stranger, has focused his attention on us. Secondly, our relationship with the Shepherd is based not on what we see, but on what we hear. We know Him because we recognize His voice. And we follow Him because we know His voice. We know that while on this earth, we cannot see God, but we can hear Him! He speaks to us through His Word, and through His Holy Spirit, even through His Creation, and we recognize His voice (I love that!).

The third thing, and maybe the most exciting, is the fact that the Shepherd calls each one of us by name! The relationship we share with Him is very personal. He knows us better than we know ourselves. This is a very special relationship we share with the Shepherd! Isaiah 49:16, **"I have engraved you on the palms of My hands."**

APPLICATION:

Take a moment to **thank** God for the privilege of being a part of His flock. Personally, I am thankful for the three

P's: His protection, His provision, and His presence! And the neat thing is, we can cultivate that relationship until it becomes richer and deeper every single day!

VERSE TO MEMORIZE:
Psalm 23 (This is a big challenge, but it will be worth it!)

Day 58

Read –
John 10:6-13

In talking about the Shepherd and His flock, Jesus now refers to Himself as the gate (or door) to the sheep pen. In Jesus' time, in that part of the world, shepherds would usually bring their sheep into a sheep pen for the night. The sheep pen was an enclosed structure without a door or gate in it. In order to protect the sheep, the shepherd would sleep in the opening to the sheep pen, thus becoming the door.

You see, sheep are not only dumb animals, they also have no known way to protect themselves. They are totally vulnerable to the dangers that stalk them. Their only protection is the shepherd. Notice here that Jesus says the sheep do not listen to those who come to harm them. The shepherd expects them to listen only to Him!

The Shepherd also compares Himself with the hired man who is hired to watch over the sheep. The hired man does fine until danger approaches, but then he runs off. Jesus says, "Not so with the shepherd." The Shepherd not only watches over His sheep, and provides for them, but He is also willing to give His life for them. Can you even imagine a shepherd who is willing to give his own life for his sheep? Well that is exactly what the Good Shepherd did for us. He gave His life that we may have life! Think of it: the Good Shepherd actually becomes the Lamb of God who takes away the sin of the world!!

APPLICATION:

So the question is: who are you listening to? Are you listening to the voices of the world and those who actually seek to harm you? Or are you listening to the Shepherd, the One who wants to protect you and provide for you? If we want to live a life that is full and meaningful, then we need to listen to the voice of the Shepherd.

VERSE TO MEMORIZE:
John 10:10

Day 59

Read – John 10:14-21

Here we have the most profound statement in the simplest of terms: **"I am the good Shepherd; I know My sheep and My sheep know Me."** (verse 14) This speaks loudly of an intimate, personal relationship with the God of the universe! And then Jesus takes it to an even higher level. He says, **"Just as the Father knows Me and I know the Father . . ."** (verse 15) And then Jesus goes on to say, not only do we know and are known, but He has come in human form to our world to actually give His life for the sheep, us!

Many scholars have wrestled with verse 16, **"I have other sheep that are not of this sheep pen. I must bring them also. They too will listen to My voice, and there shall be one flock and one shepherd."** Some believe this refers to church denominations other than our own. Others believe it refers to Christians in other cultures around the world. In either case, it refers to people who may not worship exactly like we do, but have still come to believe in Jesus the Christ. It kind of gives us a little peek into heaven. We will be surrounded by all kinds of people, like the little chorus says, "Red and yellow, black and white, they are precious in His sight. Jesus loves the little children of the world." Yes, we will all be one flock with one glorious and loving Shepherd!!

Jesus also reminds us here that in giving His life, He did it willingly and knowingly. No one took it from Him. He laid it down of His own accord. It was His choice to embrace the cross. Hebrews 12:2b says, **"who for the joy set before Him endured the cross, scorning its shame, and sat down at the right hand of the throne of God."**

I think it is very interesting here that in the last verse of this chapter, the Jews are still amazed at the healing of the man born blind, and they say, **"These are not the sayings of a man possessed by a demon. Can a demon open the eyes of the blind?"**

APPLICATION:

I would invite you to spend some time today just relishing in the fact of your relationship with the God of this universe. He is the Divine Shepherd, and we have been invited into His flock. And there has never been a shepherd who cares for his sheep like this Shepherd does. Even to the point of giving His own life that we might be redeemed. Praise Him!

VERSE TO MEMORIZE:
John 10:14

Day 60

Read – John 10:22-30

It was time for the Feast of Dedication, better known as the Festival of Hanukkah, or the Feast of Lights. It was always held close to the time of winter solstice. Jesus was there. He was walking in the temple area. It seems the Jews kind of cornered Him, and they asked Him, **"How long will You keep us in suspense? If You are the Christ, tell us plainly."** (verse 24) Now it wasn't that He hadn't told them; the issue was their refusal to believe what He had plainly told them. So He said to them, **"I did tell you, but you do not believe."** (verse 25)

Jesus has made it clear, through His miracles and His teaching, just who He is, and where He has come from, but it's not that they could not believe, rather it is that they would not believe. They refused to embrace the truth of God's revelation in Jesus. And the reason they will not believe is because they are not His sheep.

In this passage we also have the great promise of the security we have in Christ. He says to these Jews that no one can snatch those who are His out of His hand. They are secure in their relationship with Him. Now that security is still based on the freedom of choice that God created us with. We have to choose daily to follow Him. God created us with the freedom of choice. We are not puppets on a string. When we choose to believe in Christ and follow Him as our great Shepherd, we do not lose our ability to choose. It's true, no one can nullify the relationship we share with Christ. But if we so choose, we can leave by the same door through which we entered this blessed relationship, our own free will. However, it is also true that the closer you walk with the Lord the less likely and difficult it would be to choose to walk away. It's difficult, like trying to get taffy out of your teeth!

APPLICATION:

It is very clear here that what we choose to believe either opens the door to all that God wants us to know, or it closes the door to that same revelation. Jesus said here, **"My sheep listen to My voice; I know them, and they follow Me."** (verse 27) God has told us many things in His Word, but if we do not have an openness to His truth, then we will never really understand it.

VERSE TO MEMORIZE:
John 10:27

Day 61

Read – John 10:31-42

These times of dialogue the Jews have with Jesus are not healthy discussions, trying to arrive at some understanding; rather, they are founded upon a deep hatred the Jews had for Jesus. This is the third time they try to kill Him. Their intentions are clear, they want to get rid of this man called Jesus.

In this passage the Jews make it clear why they want to take His life. It is because He is guilty of blasphemy according to their law. They even define the blasphemy for which He is accused. They say, **"we are stoning You because You, a mere man, claim to be God."** At least they are clear about who Jesus claims to be. Like it has been said about Jesus, "He is either exactly who He claimed to be, or He is the greatest liar that has ever lived, because He claimed to be God."

In verses 34-38 Jesus states His defense. He says, **"I am trying to show you that I am God's Son by the miracles** that I do, for they are the works of My Father." This only heightened their animosity. In verse 39 they try to seize Him once again. But the neat thing is they will never seize Him until He Himself is willing to be seized. This again is because His time has not yet come. But the cross is on the horizon!

APPLICATION:

In our world today there is more animosity towards Christianity than at any other time in my lifetime. These people not only do not believe, they even resent your right to believe. So what is the Christian response? I believe it is always love! Love will always respect those who disagree with us. Paul tells us in Romans 12:19, **"Do not take revenge, my friends, but leave room for God's wrath, for it is written: 'It is Mine to avenge; I will repay,' says the Lord."**

VERSE TO MEMORIZE:
Romans 12:19

Day 62

Read –
John 11:1-16

Lazarus was a close friend of Jesus, as were his two sisters, Mary and Martha. They lived in the village of Bethany, only a few miles from Jerusalem. Lazarus became sick. The two sisters sent word to Jesus that their brother was *very* sick. John emphasizes the fact that Jesus loved Lazarus and his two sisters. Jesus and His disciples had stayed at their home many times.

When Jesus gets the news that Lazarus is sick, He makes the statement, **"This sickness will not end in death. No, it is for God's glory so that God's Son may be glorified through it."** (verse 4) After saying that, Jesus delays leaving for Bethany for two more days. After two days, Jesus says, "Let's go!" However, because the Jews were trying to kill Him the disciples said, **"You don't want to go back there; the Jews are trying to kill You."** (paraphrase)

According to verse 14 Jesus already knew that Lazarus was dead, even though His disciples thought Lazarus was just in a deep sleep. In fact, Jesus said to His disciples, **"I am glad I was not there (when Lazarus died), so that you may believe. But let us go to him."** (verse 15) And then the disciple who has incurred the reputation of "doubting Thomas" says, **"Let us also go, that we may die with Him."** (verse 16)

APPLICATION:

I'm so glad that we don't always have to understand what God is up to. Isaiah 55:9 says, **"As the heavens are higher than the earth, so are My ways higher than your ways and My thoughts than your thoughts."** Mary and Martha did not understand why Jesus delayed. The disciples didn't understand what Jesus was doing, or even what He said. Don't ever underestimate God, or put Him into a box. God is always at work in ways that are beyond our understanding.

VERSES TO MEMORIZE:
Isaiah 55:8-9

Day 63

Read – John 11:17-37

Before Jesus and His disciples arrived at the home of Mary and Martha, while Jesus was still on the edge of town, the sisters came to Him one at a time. Both sisters said the very same thing: **"If You had been here, my brother would not have died."** (verses 21 & 32) Jesus attempted to comfort the sisters, even weeping as they wept. He was either identifying with their sorrow, or He was weeping because He was going to bring Lazarus back from the dead. I don't know about you, but once God calls me home, I don't want to come back!

As Jesus talked with Martha He said some of the most profound words He had ever spoken. In verse 25 Jesus said to Martha, **"I am the resurrection and the life. He who believes in Me will live, even though he dies; and whoever lives and believes in Me will never die. Do you believe this?"** There's that word again, "believe." The theme of John's gospel. To believe in Jesus as the Divine Son of God is to change your eternal address to read "Heaven!" Martha's response to the words of Jesus was, **"Yes, Lord, I believe that You are the Christ, the Son of God, who was to come into the world."**

A pastor officiating at the funeral of one of his parishioners made the statement, "Well, he has completed his baptism!" Baptism is a symbol of death and resurrection.; the grave of a Christian shouts "resurrection."

APPLICATION:

The most powerful choice you will ever make in this life is the choice to believe in Jesus the Christ! It changes your life. It changes your history. It changes your eternal address. You become a new creation in Christ.

VERSES TO MEMORIZE:
John 11:25-26

Day 64

Read – John 11:38-44

Verse 38 tells us that Jesus was deeply moved by this whole situation. Even though He knew what He was going to do, He was moved by the pain experienced by those He loved. I love the words of the Hymn "Does Jesus Care." In that hymn, verse four says, "Does Jesus care when I've said 'Good Bye,' to the dearest on earth to me. And my sad heart aches till it nearly breaks? Is it aught to Him? Does He see?" And the chorus says, "Oh, yes, He cares; I know He cares. His heart is touched with my grief. When the days are weary, the long nights dreary, I know my Savior cares."

When they arrived at the grave of Lazarus, Jesus instructed them to remove the stone. They may have hesitated for a moment when Martha said, **"by this time there is a bad odor, for he has been there four days."** Then Jesus said, **"Did I not tell you that if you believed, you would see the glory of God?"** (verses 39 & 40)

Then Jesus looked up to heaven and began to pray, **"Father, I thank You that You have heard Me. I knew that You always hear Me, but I said this for the benefit of the people standing here, that they may believe that You sent Me."** (verse 41 & 42) And then Jesus said those powerful words, **"Lazarus, come out!"** Truly a powerful miracle! Some have said that if Jesus had not called Lazarus by name, the entire graveyard would have erupted in life. It was the miracle that sparked the flame that led to the cross.

APPLICATION:

If you had been there that day would you have noticed that Lazarus came out of the tomb wrapped in his grave clothes? Some believe that is actually an illustration of what happens when God calls our name as we believe and come from death to life. After our initial salvation we often are still bound by some of those things that cause temptations to come our way. Undesirable habits, moral problems, the speech we use, and other things that have been a part of our God-less lifestyle. We need for the church to help us to get rid of those grave clothes.

VERSES TO MEMORIZE:
Romans 8:1-2

Day 65

John 11:45-57

The road to the cross begins right here! Raising a man who had been in the grave for four days really got the people's attention. For some, it brought them to faith. Verse 45 tells us that many put their faith in Him. But for those who hated Jesus, who had been seeking to take His life, there was a new sense of urgency. In fact, they called a special meeting of the Sanhedrin. They were afraid because of the following Jesus was accumulating. It was going to result in action by the Roman government, and the Jews were going to lose the little they did have. For them, to allow Jesus to continue doing what He was doing meant political suicide.

The conclusion of this meeting by the Sanhedrin was that Jesus must die. He must die for the good of the Jewish nation. Little did they realize that Jesus would die, not only for the good of the Jewish nation, but for the good of all people. He was destined to be the Sacrificial Lamb, the Suffering Servant, the Hope of the world.

When Jesus realized that the end was near, He quit His public ministry. He sought for a place for He and His disciples in a small town named Ephraim. In the days that lay ahead, God's timetable for His Son would be fulfilled perfectly. About this time people began to gather in Jerusalem for the coming Passover celebration. And many of those coming to Jerusalem were looking for Jesus. But the religious leaders warned them, **"If anyone sees Jesus, he is to report it so that He might be arrested."** (verse 57)

APPLICATION:

Passover is on the horizon! Passover is the Jewish celebration of their escape from Egyptian bondage. The instructions on that fateful night was that every family would sacrifice a lamb and smear the blood over the doorposts of their homes to gain protection from the death angel. Jesus is going to become the Lamb of God, who would give His life that we might escape our bondage to sin. It is His blood that will be shed in fulfillment of this great Jewish celebration. Every time, we as believers participate in the sacrament of communion, we remember this week and all Jesus did for us.

VERSES TO MEMORIZE:
Ephesians 1:7-8

Day 66

Read – John 12:1-11

Six days before Passover Jesus and His disciples make their way to Bethany, to the home of Lazarus, Mary and Martha. A special dinner is given for Jesus and Lazarus. After dinner, Mary took some expensive perfume and poured it on Jesus' feet and then wiped them with her hair. When Judas saw this taking place, he objected. He said, **"Why wasn't this perfume sold and the money given to the poor?"** (verse 5) At this point John gives us a little insight on Judas. He tells us that Judas served as the treasurer of the group, and as such used to help himself to the money. John calls him a thief.

Now Jesus does not comment on what Judas says but He does comment on what Mary did. Jesus says, **"Leave her alone. It was intended that she should save this perfume for the day of My burial. You will always have the poor among you, but you will not always have Me."** (verses 7-8) This is the second time Jesus tells His disciples that He is going to die. He will say it again later, but it seems like they never really hear Him. There is no recorded response from them.

Now after this special dinner, and the anointing of Jesus by Mary, we learn that many more people showed up. Remember, they had been looking for Jesus and didn't know what had happened to Him. These people also wanted to see Lazarus, who had been raised from the dead. And because Lazarus had also become popular, the Jews decided to kill him as well.

APPLICATION:

Do you think we are as slow to really listen to the words of our Lord as these disciples were? They had no idea of what was ahead for them, even though Jesus had given them warning. They also had a thief in their midst whom they had not been willing to deal with. Do you see yourself in any part of this story?

VERSE TO MEMORIZE:
Psalm 119:169

Day 67

Read – John 12:12-19

This passage gives us an exceptional picture of the excitement that surrounded Jesus. It is the first day of the week and Jesus and His disciples are on their way to Jerusalem. When the people realize Jesus is on His way to Jerusalem, they cut down palm branches and lay them in the pathway of His journey. And in fulfillment of scripture, Jesus is riding on a young donkey. (Zechariah 9:9) The people who had gathered along the way begin to shout their praises to Jesus as the King of Israel.

John tells us that Jesus' disciples did not understand what was happening. Their understanding of this event didn't take place until much later. John also tells us that most of the people who had gathered along Jesus' route into Jerusalem were the same group of people who had witnessed the raising of Lazarus from the dead. Because of their testimony, the crowd continued to grow until the Pharisees exclaimed, **"See,**

this is getting us nowhere. Look how the whole world has gone after Him!" (verse 19)

APPLICATION:

Of course we know this event as the Triumphal Entry or Palm Sunday. We still celebrate it to this day! As we meditate on this event, we must realize that this is exactly what Jesus wants to do in our own lives: make His triumphal entry into our hearts and lives! When we invite Jesus to come into our lives as our Savior and Lord, there should be as much celebration in our own hearts as there was that day. Thank Him today for His grand entry into your heart and life.

VERSE TO MEMORIZE:

Revelation 3:20

(An invitation for our own personal triumphal entry)

Day 68

Read – John 12:20-36

In this passage Jesus predicts His death in words that most of the people did not understand. In verses 20-22 some Greeks, who were in Jerusalem for Passover, came to Philip and stated that they wanted to see Jesus. At this time Jesus was separating Himself from the public. He has a laser focus on the cross that is just a few days away. Philip takes the message to Andrew and both go to Jesus with the Greeks request. Jesus does not respond to this request, rather He shares with them some statements about His death.

In verse 23 (for the first time) we see the words, **"The hour has come . . ."** Up until this Jesus had said many times, **"My hour has not yet come."** Jesus goes on to illustrate His upcoming death by a kernel of wheat that must fall to the ground and die before it produces anything. And then He issues that great statement of true discipleship in verse 25: **"The man who loves his life will lose it, while the man** who hates his life in this world will keep it for eternal life."**

In verses 27-28 Jesus affirms that it was for this very hour that He came to this earth. Like the kernel of wheat, He came to die that we might live. And so now He says, **"Now My heart is troubled, and what shall I say? Father, save Me from this hour? No, it was for this very reason I came to this hour. Father, glorify Your name!"** And then a voice came from heaven (just like at His baptism) saying, **"I have glorified it, and will glorify it again."** Some heard the voice, and others thought it had thundered. And then Jesus said, **"This voice was for your benefit, not Mine."** (verse 30)

Jesus concludes this passage by sharing the method of His death by saying, **"When I am lifted up from the earth, I will draw all men to Myself."** (verse 32) He then challenges them that when darkness comes, they are to walk in the light. After that, He went into hiding.

APPLICATION:

What do we learn here? We learn why Jesus came to our world. We learn about the kind of commitment true discipleship takes. We get a glimpse of just how Jesus is going to die. And we are challenged to be children of the light. This passage contains some powerful words from our Lord. It may take a couple of days of rest on the trail, meditating on the words of Jesus, before we are ready to go on.

VERSE TO MEMORIZE:
John 12:26

Day 69

Read – John 12:37-43

Do you remember what John wrote in the very first chapter, verse 11, **"He came to that which was His own, but His own did not receive Him?"** This passage is all about the truth of that statement. Jesus truly came to His own, the Jewish people, and in their midst, He did many miracles, and shared the truth about the Kingdom of God. But they refused to receive it. So John tells us here that this is all a fulfillment of scripture. Isaiah had actually written about this rejection many years before.

And even though God has done everything possible to make Himself known to us, unless we respond to His truth we bring condemnation to ourselves. That's what happens when God has created us with the privilege of self-choice. We have the ability to reject God's divine plan for His children. So when we choose darkness over light, we truly walk in the darkness. Our spiritual eyes are unwilling to see, and our hearts become dead to God's truth.

John also tells us here that many of the religious leaders did choose to believe in Jesus as the Christ. But they found themselves faced with another problem: rejection by their peers. So what did they do? They did not live out their faith! John says here, **"they loved praise from men more than praise from God."** (verse 43)

APPLICATION:

We love it when others think well of us, but when that causes us to hide our witness, then we are in trouble. For the utmost goal of our lives should be to receive praise from God. Above all, I want to please my Lord and Savior! Is that your goal too?

VERSE TO MEMORIZE:
I Peter 2:9

Day 70

Read – John 12:44-50

Here Jesus honors the Father, who is the One who sent Him into our world. When we honor Jesus we honor the Father, and vice versa. When we refuse to honor God in any way, we bring judgment upon ourselves. Jesus says here in verse 47, **"As for the person who hears My words but does not keep them, I do not judge him. For I did not come to judge the world, but to save it."** But there is judgment, and that judgment comes in the words of Jesus that we have rejected. When we reject the words of Jesus we are choosing darkness over light. Jesus said back in John 3:19, **"This is the verdict: Light has come into the world, but men loved darkness instead of light because their deeds were evil."**

When we reject the words of Jesus we are rejecting the words of the Father, for Jesus only speaks what the Father tells Him to speak. Verse 50 ends by saying, **"I know that His

command leads to eternal life. So whatever I say is just what the Father has told Me to say."

APPLICATION:

We must always take God's Word seriously! The words God speaks are not negotiable. We do not have the right to decide whether they are true for us or not. They are always true! In Him there is no falsehood.

VERSE TO MEMORIZE:

Psalm 119:11

Day 71

Read – John 13:1-17

We are moving quickly to the end of our trek through John's gospel. While the other gospels focus on the disciples preparation for the Passover meal, John's focus is on all that Jesus said during the time they are gathered together in the Upper Room. The first thing Jesus does is wash the disciples feet. Because the streets were dusty and the people wore sandals, it was customary for the host to provide for the washing of the feet of a guest.

I love the second part of verse 1; **"Having loved His own who were in the world, He now showed them the full extent of His love."** How did Jesus do that? By washing their feet? By sharing with them the sacrament of His broken body and shed blood? By dying on the cross? I believe it is all of the above!

When Jesus began to prepare Himself for the washing of the disciple's feet, Peter stopped Him. Peter said, **"You shall never wash my feet."** Jesus said, **"Unless I do, you have no part with Me."** And Peter responded, **"Then Lord, not just my feet but my hands and my head as well!"** Peter was saying, "If this is the plan, then I want all of it!" This is in direct contrast to the attitude of Judas who was planning to betray Jesus on this night. One wonders what Judas was feeling as Jesus stooped down to wash his feet?

When Jesus finished washing the feet of His disciples He began to use this event to teach them the truth about servanthood. In essence Jesus says to them, **"There is no greater calling than to be a servant one to another."** (paraphrase) And Jesus concluded by saying, **"Now that you know these things, you will be blessed if you do them."** (verse 17)

APPLICATION:

Now here we are some two thousand years later, and most people still do not understand the beauty of servanthood. There is a special blessing for those who serve others. Some people interpret what Jesus said to infer that we need the ritual of washing feet today. But that is not His message. It is not in the ritual but in the service we give to one another.

Today there are still churches that practice the ritual of foot washing. The only problem is, most people come to those rituals with clean feet!

VERSE TO MEMORIZE:
Galatians 5:13

Day 72

Read – John 13:18-30

In this passage Jesus confides in His disciples that one of them is going to betray Him. He says to them, **"I am telling you now before it happens, so that when it does happen you will believe that I am He."** (verse 19) Then in verse 21 Jesus makes it very clear. He says, **"I tell you the truth, one of you is going to betray Me."** The disciples all looked at each other, afraid to ask Jesus. **Finally Peter motions to John and says, "Ask Him which one He means." So John says to Jesus, "Lord, is it I?" And Jesus answered, "It is the one to whom I will give this piece of bread when I have dipped it in the dish."** (verses 22-25)

This moment is not the communion sacrament. It is thought that before he singled Judas out, Jesus had shared with them the bread and the cup as His broken body and shed blood. So when He handed this piece of bread to Judas, it is the very bread that had served as an illustration of His broken body.

And as Jesus gave the bread to Judas, He says, **"What you are about to do, do quickly."** John records that the disciples had no idea what Judas was to "do quickly."

This passage ends with verse 30 which says, **"As soon as Judas had taken the bread, he went out. And it was night."** Yes, it was night, in more ways than one!

APPLICATION:

It is a terrible thing to betray someone. It is doubly bad when the one betrayed is one who loves you deeply. Judas always had an eye for money. I believe he thought that by betraying Jesus he would force Jesus to perform a great miracle that would usher in His Kingdom. How wrong he was!

VERSE TO MEMORIZE:
II Timothy 1:14

Day 73

Read – John 13:31-38

This passage is actually an introduction to chapter 14. The entire 14th chapter of John's gospel is the response of Jesus to four interruptions. Those interruptions begin here in the end of the 13th chapter. Jesus and His disciples are still in the upper room. Jesus is speaking to them about what is ahead. He says to them, **"Now is the Son of Man glorified . . .My children, I will be with you only a little longer . . . A new command I give you: Love one another."** (verses 31-34)

Most of us have been in a setting where the teacher has said something that really grabbed our attention but when the teacher went on to a new subject, we were still thinking about what he had said earlier. That's what happens here. Jesus talks about being glorified, then He tells the disciples He is going away. Then He begins to talk to them about loving each other. But all Peter heard was that Jesus was going to go away, and they would not be able to follow Him. So, as

Jesus is talking about love, Peter says, **"Lord, where are You going?"** (verse 36) This is the first of the four interruptions. And the answer to Peter's question comes in the first four verses of chapter 14.

Now, Peter really did love the Lord! He verbalized it often. And when Jesus tells him that he will be unable to follow wherever Jesus is going, Peter says in verse 37, **"Lord, why can't I follow You now? I will lay down my life for You."** But Jesus responds with **"You just think you will lay down your life for me. The truth is, you are going to deny Me three times before the rooster crows in the morning."** (paraphrase)

APPLICATION:

It is so easy to tell God those things we believe He wants to hear from us. We even sing about how committed we are to the Lord. But in reality, often when the chips are down, we fail to carry through with our commitments. We need to make sure that our lifestyle matches what we are so quick to verbalize or sing about. Our walk needs to match our talk!

VERSES TO MEMORIZE:

John 13:34-35

Day 74

John 14:1-4

"Do not let your hearts be troubled. Trust in God; trust also in Me. In My Father's house are many rooms; if it were not so, I would have told you. I am going there to prepare a place for you. And if I go and prepare a place for you, I will come back and take you to be with Me that you also may be where I am. You know the way to the place where I am going."

The words that Jesus speaks here are a direct answer to Peter's question in 13:36. Jesus is saying to Peter, **"Don't be troubled. I am going away, but I am going so I might prepare a place for you to be with Me for all eternity. And after that I will return for you so that we will be together forever. And in reality, you know the way to where I am going."** (paraphrase)

These are some of the most quoted words in the Bible. They are words of comfort and optimism. These words are spoken to us as much as they are to Peter. These words tell us about all that we have to look forward to. Jesus is personally involved in preparing for our arrival in heaven. And we know that it will be beyond anything we could ever imagine. All of this is a part of that great hope that the Bible tells us is ours. I love what Paul writes in Romans 15:12, **"May the God of hope fill you with all joy and peace as you trust in Him, so that you may overflow with hope by the power of the Holy Spirit."**

APPLICATION:

I memorized these verses years ago in the King James Version of the Bible where it says, **"In My Father's house are many mansions . . . "** (verse 2) Then when the New International Version came out, and it said, **"In My Father's house are many rooms . . ."** I was devastated. We have been downsized from a mansion to a room. But the truth of the matter is, God's plan is all about relationships, and He wants us to be all together. I really don't know what that looks like, but whatever it is it will be wonderful!

VERSES TO MEMORIZE:

John 14:2-3 (Also Romans 15:12)

Day 75

John 14:5-7

"Thomas said to Him, 'Lord, we don't know where You are going, so how can we know the way?' Jesus answered, 'I am the way and the truth and the life. No one comes to the Father except through Me. If you really knew Me, you would know My Father as well. From now on, you do know Him and have seen Him.'"

This is the second of the four interruptions. When Thomas heard Jesus say, **"You know the way to the place where I am going,"** he thought, "we don't even know where He is going, how can we know the way?" I think it was somewhat difficult for these early disciples to really grasp that Jesus was really God! I love what the writer of Hebrews says in chapter 1, verse 3, **"The Son is the radiance of God's glory and the exact representation of His being, sustaining all things by His powerful word."**

In answering Thomas Jesus gives us another powerful statement. He says, **"I am the way and the truth and the life. No one comes to the Father except through Me."** In essence Jesus is saying, **"I am everything you will ever need; everything you are seeking in this life. And the only way to really know God the Father is through a relationship with Me!"** (paraphrase)

APPLICATION:

There are many people in our world today who tell us that there are many ways to get to God, and all of them are equally effective. Jesus says that is not true. Are we going to choose to believe Jesus, or the world? To believe in Christ is to believe every word that He ever said. So much of people's religion is based on theory, but true Christianity is based on a personal relationship, and His actual words!

VERSE TO MEMORIZE:
John 14:6

Day 76

Read –
John 14:8-14

The third interruption comes through Philip. It's in the form of a statement. Philip said, **"Lord, show us the Father and that will be enough for us."** Jesus gives a short answer. He says, **"Anyone who has seen Me has seen the Father."** But when Jesus goes on to expand on His answer, it all comes back to that word "believe." Jesus says to Philip, **"Don't you believe that I am in the Father, and that the Father is in Me?"**

Jesus says something else here that some people have trouble with. He says in verses 12-14, **"I tell you the truth, anyone who has faith in Me will do what I have been doing. He will do even greater things than these, because I am going to the Father. And I will do whatever you ask in My name, so that the Son may bring glory to the Father. You may ask Me for anything in My name, and I will do it."**

This sounds like a blank check for anything we may want. It is much broader than that. When Jesus returned to the Father He gave birth to the Church. The Church is to be the very hands and feet of Christ. On any given day, around the world, the gospel is being preached and miracles are taking place in greater measure than what Jesus could do while He was here as just one Person. And these days God uses the miraculous differently than when Jesus was here.

Then Jesus says, **"You may ask Me for anything in My name, and I will do it."** What does He mean by **"in My name?"** Whatever we ask must come under His authority and according to His will. God is not some automat that if we push the right buttons we can always get our way. That would make God less than God!

APPLICATION:

This whole issue comes down to the sovereignty of God. He is always the One in charge. Even when He answers prayer, sometimes the answer is "yes" and sometimes it is "no," and sometimes it is "wait." We are to be submissive and committed to His will in everything.

VERSES TO MEMORIZE:
I John 5:14-15

Day 77

Read – John 14:15-21

At this point Jesus begins to teach His disciples about the Holy Spirit. He makes it clear in this passage that even though He is going away He is sending them the Holy Spirit. In verse 16 He says, **"And I will ask the Father, and He will give you another Counselor to be with you forever."** When Jesus uses the word "another" He has two options, for there are two different meanings for the word "another." One use means "another of a different kind." The second use means "another of the same kind." What Jesus used here is "another of the same kind." In other words, the Holy Spirit will be to us just like Jesus! He will be our counselor. He will be our truth.

This third Person of the divine Godhead is not only going to be with us, He is going to live in us. Jesus says in verse 20, **"On that day you will realize that I am in My Father, and you are in Me, and I am in you."** What a dynamic relationship! Jesus also tells His disciples that this is to be a "love relationship." Because we love Him, we will obey His commands. And because He loves us, He will reveal Himself to us in new and refreshing ways.

APPLICATION:

To understand the ministry of the Holy Spirit is crucial to a victorious walk with Jesus! The Holy Spirit has been called "God in the present tense." In other words, He is the One who makes God real to us. He is the One who guides us into all truth. He is the One who empowers us to do God's will. We need to learn how to talk to Him and listen to Him every single day. Do it while you work. Do it while you wait in line. Do it as you drive your vehicle. He is always accessible.

VERSE TO MEMORIZE:
John 14:21

Day 78

Read – John 14:22-31

The fourth interruption comes from Judas (not Iscariot). He asks, **"But Lord, why do You intend to show Yourself to us and not to the world?"** You see, Judas had been listening to Jesus tell about how, through the Holy Spirit, He is going to reveal Himself to us. And yet the disciples know that the great plan of God is really for the whole world. So in revealing Himself, why would He leave out the world? I think that is a great question!

In essence Jesus says in His response, **"If you really love Me, you will obey Me, and We are going to make our home in you. But if you don't love Me, and don't obey My words, then you have chosen against having a relationship with Us! Besides that, if you do love Me, the Holy Spirit is going to continue to teach you My truth. He will remind you of everything I have told you."** (paraphrase)

And then in verse 27 Jesus says to these disciples, **"Peace I leave with you; My peace I give you. I do not give to you as the world gives. Do not let your hearts be troubled and do not be afraid."** The same words Jesus spoke at the beginning of this chapter: **"Do not let your hearts be troubled."** Those are wonderful words for us to hear in our day and age.

In verse 28 Jesus says, **"If you loved Me, you would be glad that I am going to the Father . . . "** Why should they be glad that Jesus is leaving? Because it opens to us all that is a part of the New Covenant God is initiating with His people. No longer does the Spirit of God dwell in holy places; now He dwells in Holy people. Jesus ends this passage with the words **"Come now; let us leave."**

APPLICATION:

This section says a lot about how God makes Himself known to us. It says a lot about the intimacy of our relationship with Him. Let us learn how to live our lives with a constant awareness of His presence within us.

VERSE TO MEMORIZE:
John 14:27

Day 79

Read – John 15:1-8

As we have been hiking through John's gospel, have you noticed all of the fruit trees and the grape vines growing in this part of the world? Jesus is very good at taking what is familiar to His disciples and using it to illustrate spiritual truth. In this passage Jesus uses the grape vines that abound in this part of the world. These disciples know all about how grape vines grow, but do they know the spiritual lesson that Jesus is giving them?

In this illustration God the Father is the gardener who tends to His vines, of which we are a part of. One of the jobs of the gardener is to prune the vines so they can become more fruitful. That means God wants to eliminate everything in our lives that is a hindrance to our ability to bear fruit.

Jesus also tells us that no branch can bear fruit of itself, it must be connected to the vine. And Jesus is that Vine!

Verse 5 is really a promise to us: **"I am the Vine; you are the branches. If a man remains in Me and I in him, he will bear much fruit; apart from Me you can do nothing."** Our fruitfulness ultimately depends on the health of the relationship we share with Jesus! And Jesus makes it clear that if we do not remain in Him, we are like those branches that are cut off and thrown into the fire.

There is another wonderful promise in verses 7-8, **"If you remain in Me and My words remain in you, ask whatever you wish, and it will be given you. This is to My Father's glory, that you bear much fruit, showing yourselves to be My disciples."**

APPLICATION:

It is God's divine plan that we not only share in a special relationship with Him, but that we be fruitful in that relationship. What does it mean to be a fruit-bearing disciple? I think it means that we are reproducing ourselves as followers of Jesus Christ. The witness we share, the service we give, our stewardship of His resources, all serve to create fruit for the kingdom.

VERSE TO MEMORIZE:

John 15:5

Day 80

Read – John 15:9-17

Jesus reminds us here that the relationship we share with Him is a love relationship. It is based on His love for us and our love for Him. Remember when Jesus gave us the Great Commandment, the commandment that is the foundation for all the other commandments. We find it in Matthew 22:37, **"Love the Lord your God with all your heart and with all your soul and with all your mind."** And when we really love Him it is easy to obey His commandments.

In verse 11 Jesus says, **"I have told you this so that My joy may be in you and that your joy may be complete."** *Joy* is one of my favorite words in the Bible. In verse 13 Jesus reminds us that if we really love Him, then we will surely love those around us. He reminds us of just how special this relationship is that we have with Him. He says in verse 15, **"I no longer call you servants, because a servant does not know his master's business. Instead, I have called you** friends, for everything that I learned from My Father I have made known to you."

APPLICATION:

Think about all that Jesus is teaching us in this passage. First of all, that He really loves us. Secondly, He wants us to love Him and to obey His commandments. He considers us to be His friends who are privy to His revelations that He gives us daily. He also wants us to live our lives in the center of a great joy that comes from Him. And He wants us to love each other with the same kind of love He has for us. Then, Jesus wraps up this passage with the words of verse 16, **"You did not choose Me, but I chose you and appointed you to go and bear fruit – fruit that will last."** That is a lot of stuff in this short passage. You could meditate on this for a couple of days. Also, if you live in Northwest Oregon as I do, everywhere you go you will see grape vines: let them be reminders of Jesus words to us.

VERSE TO MEMORIZE:
John 15:16

Day 81

Read –
John 15:18-16:4

In the last passage Jesus said a lot of things about love, but now He turns in the opposite direction and talks to us about hate. Jesus does not want us to be ignorant of the reality that there are many people in the world who actually hate Him. He tells us that because they hate Him, they will hate us also. This is true. There will be times when we will encounter people who may not openly hate Jesus and His Church, but will choose to ignore us and belittle the relationship we have with Jesus.

In the first part of chapter 16 Jesus even tells His disciples that they can be killed for their faith in Jesus. In fact, those who would kill actually believe they are doing God a favor. He says in verse 4, **"I have told you this, so that when the time comes you will remember that I warned you. I did not tell you this at first because I was with you."**

John does end chapter 15 on a positive note as Jesus shares with His disciples in verse 26, **"When the Counselor comes, whom I will send to you from the Father, the Spirit of truth who goes out from the Father, He will testify about Me."** The Holy Spirit is really the key to having victory in any and all situations that we may face. He will always guide us into all truth.

The last verse in this chapter is a challenge to the disciples, and to us. Jesus says to them, **"And you also must testify, for you have been with Me from the beginning."** Jesus always has a word to say to our generation, and we have been challenged to share His message with our world. Even though our world might not readily receive it, it is a powerful word and will accomplish its purpose. Isaiah 55:11 says, **"My word that goes out from My mouth will not return to Me empty, but will accomplish what I desire and achieve the purpose for which I sent it."**

APPLICATION:

The hate that Jesus talks about seems to be more prevalent in certain parts of the world. However, none of us are immune from encountering animosity in various degrees. How do we handle it? We remember that they hated Him before they hated us. And He has given us the Holy Spirit, who lives within us and who guides us into all truth. Those early disciples faced times of testing, and we will, too. But let us learn how to depend on the wisdom and power of the Holy Spirit.

VERSE TO MEMORIZE:
John 15:13

Day 82

Read – John 16:5-16

In this passage Jesus continues His teaching on the Holy Spirit. In reality, the Holy Spirit is the Spirit of Jesus which was given to us after Jesus returned to the Father. And for the second time Jesus says to His disciples in verse 7, **"I tell you the truth: It is for your good that I am going away. Unless I go away, the Counselor (Holy Spirit) will not come to you; but if I go, I will send Him to you."**

The Holy Spirit has a two-pronged ministry in this world. First of all, He comes to convict the world of sin, of righteousness, and of judgment. He convicts of sin when we refuse to believe in God's remedy for sin. He convicts of righteousness when we really see the righteousness that was in Jesus. And He convicts of judgment because the prince of this world, old Satan himself, stands condemned.

The second part of the Holy Spirit's ministry is in the promise Jesus gives that the Spirit will guide us into all truth. I love verse 14, **"He will bring glory to Me by taking from what is Mine and making it known to you."** It is almost impossible to comprehend how much God wants to reveal Himself to His children!

The teaching that Jesus shares with His disciples in chapters 14, 15 and 16 are called The Farewell Discourses. His teaching here is so powerful that we ought to spend a few days just re-reading and meditating on all He says.

APPLICATION:

Take up the challenge to really understand all that the Holy Spirit brings to this relationship we share with the Lord. In many churches the Holy Spirit is the misunderstood Deity of the Godhead. The real challenge is, not only to know about Him, but to experience His power in our lives.

VERSES TO MEMORIZE:

John 16:14-15

Day 83

Read – John 16:17-28

I love those times when we are able to get a little glimpse into the human nature of the disciples. This is one place where that is true. The disciples are talking among themselves and they are asking, **"What does Jesus mean by saying, 'In a little while you will see Me no more, and then after a little while you will see Me."** If I had been there I probably would have asked the same question. What in the world does Jesus mean by "a little while?"

Jesus became aware of the question the disciples were asking, so He explained it to them. His answer points to the Resurrection. He shares with them that there will be a time of grief, followed by great joy. He uses the birth of a baby to illustrate how pain is transferred into great joy when the baby arrives. The crucifixion of Jesus will create great pain for the disciples. They will be filled with grief and with fear. But three days later will come a joy that is greater than anyone can imagine. In the second part of verse 20 Jesus says, **"You will grieve, but your grief will turn to joy."** It is interesting that Jesus doesn't say that their sorrow will be replaced with joy, but their grief will turn to joy. Their sorrow actually becomes their source of joy!

Jesus knows that these disciples are really not ready for all the gory details. So He says to them in verse 25, **"Though I have been speaking figuratively, a time is coming when I will no longer use this kind of language but will tell you plainly about My Father."** Jesus always wants us to know the truth—when we are ready.

APPLICATION:

Like the disciples, we will have times when we are not ready to hear the answers to our questions. Like Charles Albert Tindley's old hymn says, "We will understand it better by and by." But now is when we need the patience that only God can give us. Like when a woman is weaving a quilt, the underside looks like a mess, but on the top side we see the beauty of that quilt. While we are living this life, the underside is all we are able to see. But one day it will all be made clear! It is then that our joy will be made complete.

VERSE TO MEMORIZE:

John 16:33

Day 84

Read – John 16:29-33

The greatest four words in this passage are in verse 31, **"You believe at last!"** That is a far cry from what Jesus had asked them so many times, **"Do you still have no faith?"** Here they are, gathered together on the night Jesus will face the cross. Jesus has shared with them the emblems of His broken body and shed blood. He has given them some great teaching on the Holy Spirit. And now He hears their simple statement of faith, **"Now we can see that You know all things and that You do not even need to have anyone ask You questions. This makes us believe that You came from God."** (verse 30)

But immediately after affirming their statement of faith, Jesus gives them the bad news. In essence, Jesus says to them, **"I am glad for your statement of faith, but I want you to know, some difficult days are still ahead for you. But in the midst of all the difficulties I want you to have peace, My peace!"** (paraphrase)

Remember the last words of chapter 14 when Jesus says, **"Come now; let us leave."** Most biblical scholars think Jesus and His disciples left the upper room and headed for the Garden of Gethsemane. So what Jesus says to them in chapters 15 & 16 are on the way to the Garden. Now we have before us chapter 17, which is the High Priestly Prayer of Jesus that He prayed somewhere between the upper room and the Garden of Gethsemane.

APPLICATION:

In chapter 16 Jesus has talked to the disciples about Joy and about Peace. These are two very important words that are a vital part of our relationship with Him. These two things don't come to us as a part of our circumstances. They are gifts from the Father, given to us in spite of our circumstances. No matter how bad things get, God has promised us His joy and His peace. Learn to claim them, and then to thank Him for these wonderful gifts.

VERSE TO MEMORIZE:
Psalm 5:11

Day 85

John 17:1-5

"After Jesus said this, He looked toward heaven and prayed: 'Father, the time has come. Glorify Your Son, that Your Son may glorify You. For You granted Him authority over all people that He might give eternal life to all those You have given Him. Now this is eternal life: that they may know You, the only true God, and Jesus Christ, whom You have sent. I have brought You glory on earth by completing the work You gave Me to do. And now, Father, glorify Me in Your presence with the glory I had with You before the world began.'"

There are three sections to Jesus' prayer. In verses 1-5 Jesus prays for Himself; in verses 6-19 Jesus prays for His disciples; and in verses 20-26 Jesus prays for all believers.

In the first section where Jesus prays for Himself, there are two verses that really stand out for me. Verse 3, **"Now this is** eternal life: that they may know You, the only true God, and Jesus Christ whom You have sent." The gift of eternal life is in the relationship we share with Jesus. He wants us to really know Him, not merely to know about Him. And in order to know anyone we must spend time with them and communicate with them. We need to know what gives them sorrow and what gives them joy. And in knowing someone it is always a growing relationship. The more we invest in it the greater the relationship.

The second verse that stands out to me is verse 4, **"I have brought You glory on earth by completing the work You gave Me to do."** Jesus completed everything the Father had given Him to do. That is an awesome statement! Was everything done that needed to be done? No! Was God's great plan of salvation for His world completed? No! But Jesus had fulfilled what He had come to do. Wouldn't it be amazing if when we came to the end of our lives that we could say, "Lord, I have fulfilled Your plan for My life. I have done what You commissioned me to do." It almost sounds like Paul's testimony in II Timothy 4:7, **"I have fought the good fight, I have finished the race, I have kept the faith."**

APPLICATION:

Are you growing in your relationship with Jesus? Are you getting to know Him better and better every day? Are you living in fulfillment of His will in your life?

VERSES TO MEMORIZE:
II Timothy 4:7-8

Day 86

Read – John 17:6-19

In this section Jesus prays for His disciples. Jesus makes it clear in verse 9 that He is praying for His disciples: **"I pray for them. I am not praying for the world, but for those You have given Me, for they are Yours."** Jesus also says, **"And glory has come to Me through them."** The disciples have been a source of glory for Jesus! That's an awesome thought! Do we bring glory to Jesus by the way we live our lives?

Jesus also prays for their protection and for their unity. Verse 11: **"I will remain in the world no longer, but they are still in the world, and I am coming to You. Holy Father, protect them by the power of Your name – the name You gave Me – so that they may be one as we are one."**

Jesus also prays that they may have His joy within them in verse 13, and again for their protection in verse 15. So if we were to sum it all up, Jesus is praying for His disciples that they may have His joy within them; that they may be protected in this evil world, and that they may have unity as they minister together. And lastly, Jesus prays that they may be sanctified in verses 16-19. That word "sanctification" actually has two meanings: to be cleansed or purified, and secondly to be set apart for holy use.

APPLICATION:

This section reveals the heart Jesus had for His disciples. He loved them beyond measure. But at the same time we need to realize that everything He prayed for His disciples, He desires these same things for us. He desires that we live in joy and peace and in unity with one another.

VERSES TO MEMORIZE:

John 17:15-16

Day 87

Read – John 17:20-26

In this section Jesus prays for all believers. He says in verses 20-21, **"My prayer is not for them alone. I pray also for those who will believe in Me through their message, that all of them may be one, Father, just as You are in Me and I am in You."** In this passage the number one thing Jesus is praying for is unity among all believers. I think of what Jesus said while they were still in the upper room, in chapter 13 verse 35, **"By this all men will know that you are My disciples, if you love one another."** And Jesus echoes that here in verse 23, **"May they be brought to complete unity to let the world know that You sent Me and have loved them even as You have loved Me."**

Now there are many people who believe that there is no unity among believers because of the many denominations that exist in Christianity. I disagree. The worst thing that could happen is that we would have one world church. That would just invite political corruption within the Church. I love to see how the many denominations work together in sharing the gospel message with our world. They may all have a different emphasis, but when it comes to the fundamentals of our faith, they stand in agreement. Yes, there is a spiritual unity among believers that is much greater than any political unity we might have.

Jesus ends His High Priestly Prayer with these words in verse 26, **"I have made You known to them, and will continue to make You known in order that the love You have for Me may be in them and that I Myself may be in them."**

APPLICATION:

Do you enjoy the fellowship we can share with believers from other denominations? Do you enjoy working on mission projects with believers from other denominations? We really need to do much more together so that our world can see the unity that is there. The world only sees Jesus in us if we work together.

VERSES TO MEMORIZE:
John 17:22-23

Day 88

Read – John 18:1-11

At this point in our trek through the gospel of John we are on the threshold of Jesus' crucifixion and resurrection. It is Thursday night of Passion Week. In this passage Jesus and His disciples arrive in the Garden of Gethsemane. There was a place within this Garden where Jesus had often met with His disciples. Judas was aware of that place and so it is to that place that he brings a detachment of soldiers along with some of the Jewish religious leaders.

Twice, when Jesus asked this throng of oppressors **"Who is it you want,"** they replied **"Jesus of Nazareth."** Twice He replied, **"I am He."** When Jesus said, "I am He," they fell to the ground. In John's gospel we have learned about the great "I Am" sayings of Jesus, and here we see the great power that is in the statement, **"I Am He!"**

As Simon Peter watched all that was happening he decided someone needed to be Jesus' defender, so he drew his sword and cut off the ear of the servant of the high priest, whose name was Malchus. Jesus responded by rebuking Peter, and healing the ear of the servant. In His rebuke of Peter Jesus said, **"Shall I not drink the cup the Father has given Me?"** Can you just see Jesus stoop down and pick up the severed ear from off the ground, placing it back on the side of Malchus' head? The focus of Jesus was not on self-defense but on fulfilling the great plan of the Father by becoming the supreme sacrifice.

APPLICATION:

As believers we need to understand that it is not necessary for us to defend our Lord. All power in heaven and on earth has been given to Him. He knows how to defend Himself. However, He does want us to be His witnesses. He wants us to be faithful in sharing the gospel message with our world. Remember, the Word of God is our weapon: it is the sword of the Spirit. It does not have to be defended, only used. If someone were to break into your home, and you had a gun to defend yourself, and they said to you, "I don't believe in guns." You wouldn't defend your gun, you would just use it!

VERSES TO MEMORIZE:
II Corinthians 10:3-4

Day 89

Read –
John 18:12-18

After Jesus was arrested He was taken to Annas, who was a former high priest, but now the father-in-law of the present high priest, Caiaphas. Caiaphas was the one who had suggested earlier that it would be good if a man would die for the people.

As Jesus was taken to the courtyard of the high priest both Peter and John followed. John had some clout with the Jewish authorities so he was let in, and then he vouched for Peter who then was also let into the courtyard. A girl, standing at the door, said to Peter, **"You are not one of His disciples, are you?"** To which Peter answered, **"I am not."** This was Peter's first denial.

Let's get a clear picture of what is happening here. On this same night, in the upper room, Peter had said to Jesus, **"Lord, I will lay down my life for You."** (13:37) Then later, in the garden, Peter drew his sword to defend Jesus from His enemies. Peter is also the first of the disciples who had declared, **"Truly You are the Son of God."** But Jesus knew Peter better than Peter knew himself. And so He had told Peter that he would deny Jesus three times before the rooster crowed the next morning. And now it was coming to pass.

APPLICATION:

We can learn a lot from what happened to Peter. It is so easy for us to say words of commitment to our Lord, but when the chips are down what do we say; what do we do? In the context of the church, we can be so bold in our statement of allegiance to our Lord, but what about those times when we are faced with opportunities to speak for Christ in the presence of His detractors: what do we do then? Jesus knew Peter through and through; He also knows us better than we know ourselves. So let us learn to lean on the strength He gives us, and not on the mere strength we have in ourselves.

VERSES TO MEMORIZE:

Proverbs 28:1 and Hebrews 13:6

Day 90

Read –
John 18:19-27

As Jesus is questioned by the former high priest, Jesus affirms that everything that has been a part of His ministry has all been done out in the open. Nothing has been hidden. He has been very transparent with all He has said and done. In the middle of the questioning one of the officials struck Jesus in the face, accusing Him of sarcasm in His answers to the high priest. It is at this point that Annas sends Jesus to the current high priest, Caiaphas.

Now we see Peter in the courtyard of the high priest, warming himself by the fire. Once more he is accused of being one of Jesus' disciples. Again Peter denies that he is a follower of Jesus. This is his second denial. And then John gives us an interesting side note. Peter's third accuser is none other than a relative of Malchus, the one whose ear was cut off by Peter in the garden. He says to Peter, **"Didn't I see you with Him in the olive grove?"** And for the third time, Peter denied that he was with Jesus. And immediately a rooster crowed. Jesus words had been proven true!

APPLICATION:

After Peter's third denial and the rooster crowed, Peter was devastated. He knew that he had failed his Lord. And the crowing of a rooster will forever be a reminder of his failure. In that day and age, almost everyone had chickens. Every morning Peter would awaken to a reminder of his failure. Every one of us, if we are judged by our past, will flunk. We have all failed at one time or another. What is it that reminds you of your failure? It may be something we see, or something we hear, or even something we smell. We need to realize that Satan tries to use those reminders of our failure to create defeat in our present lives. Don't listen to him! It is in those times that we need to say, **"Get thee behind me, Satan!"** (Mark 8:33)

VERSES TO MEMORIZE:

Psalm 40:12-13

Day 91

Read – John 18:28-40

In this mockery of a trial Jesus has now appeared before Annas and Caiaphas, and now Caiaphas sends Him to the Roman governor, Pilate. Pilate's question is, **"What has this man done? What crime has He committed?"** After hearing the accusations, Pilate responds, **"Take Him yourselves and judge Him by your own law."** But the problem was the Jews had no authority to put anyone to death no matter what they had done. Only the Romans could carry out a sentence of death.

So because the Jews were demanding the death penalty, Pilate had Jesus brought to him inside the palace. Pilate's first question was, **"Are You king of the Jews?"** It's interesting how many times Jesus responds to His questioners with a question of His own. We can learn something from that. Maybe instead of demanding that others listen to our truth, we should ask more questions, and then be willing to listen to what they want to say. Much can be said about being good listeners!

So when Pilate asked Jesus whether He was the king of the Jews, Jesus responded, **"Is that your own idea, or did others talk to you about Me?"** And then Jesus proceeds to plead guilty as to being a king. He says to Pilate, **"My kingdom is not of this world. If it were, My servants would fight to prevent My arrest by the Jews. But now My kingdom is from another place."** Pilate says, **"You are a king, then!"** And in His response Jesus gives us a statement on the very reason He has come to our world. He says, **"You are right in saying I am a king. In fact, for this reason I was born, and for this I came into the world, to testify to the truth."**

Pilate then goes back out to the Jews and says, **"I find no basis for a charge against Him."** And then, trying to find a reason to get out of this whole mess, Pilate offers to release someone from criminal charges as was the custom during the Passover, thinking they would choose Jesus. But they didn't; they chose Barabbas, a thief and an insurrectionist.

APPLICATION:

It is never wrong to do the right thing. Pilate wanted to protect his own hide, so he chose to do the wrong thing. The truth of all this is the fact that Jesus makes His appearance in front of all of us. What will we do with Jesus the Christ? Will we embrace His truth, or will we send Him away? Don't let Him die in vain for your sin!

VERSE TO MEMORIZE:
Joshua 24:15

Day 92

Read – John 19:1-16

As we near the end of our hike through the gospel of John, the trail looks grim. The crucifixion of Jesus is an ugly thing. In this chapter, Pilate has Jesus flogged, the soldiers place a crown of thorns on His head, and clothe Him with a purple robe. All of this is a mockery to His claim to be a king. Verse 3 says that the soldiers shout out, **"Hail, king of the Jews!"** And they strike Him over and over again.

And once Jesus is beaten and bloodied, Pilate brings Him out to the people and proclaims, **"Look, I am bringing Him out to you to let you know that I find no basis for a charge against Him . . . Here is the man!"** Pilate was hoping for some sympathy for Jesus from the crowd, but none came. The Jewish religious leaders shouted all the more, **"Crucify Him! Crucify Him!"** So Pilate once again has Jesus brought before him, and he asks Jesus, **"Where do You come from?"** Jesus was silent. Pilate asks, **"Don't You realize I have power** either to set You free or to crucify You?"** Jesus answered, **"You would have no power over Me if it were not given to you from above."** Pilate once again took Jesus out in front of the people and exclaimed, **"Here is your king!"**

To apply a little more pressure, the people shouted to Pilate, **"We have no king but Caesar, and if you don't crucify this man you are setting yourself up above Caesar."** (paraphrase) And finally Pilate relents and turns Jesus over to be crucified.

APPLICATION:

Pilate found himself in a very difficult situation. He chose to do what was politically expedient. All of us will face situations where it will not be easy to do the right thing. Too many people look for the easy way out, but the cost will always be great. We need always to ask the question, "What is the right thing to do?" And I believe if we will sincerely do that, God will give us wisdom to know what the right thing is.

VERSE TO MEMORIZE:
Proverbs 11:3

Day 93

Read – John 19:16-27

This passage reveals the agony of the crucifixion. John does not go into as much detail as some of the other gospel writers, but it's still an ugly ordeal. Rather than focus on the physical pain, John talks about the sign Pilate made that was placed on the cross. It read, **"Jesus of Nazareth, the king of the Jews."** It was written in three languages; Aramaic, Latin and Greek. The Jews recoiled at calling Jesus "king of the Jews," so they wanted Pilate to change the sign to read, "He called himself king of the Jews." But Pilate refused.

This passage also tells about the soldiers gambling for Jesus' clothes, which is the fulfillment of an Old Testament scripture, Psalm 22:18. John also tells us who was at the cross. There were three Marys; Mary, Jesus' mother, His mother's sister, Mary, wife of Clopas, Mary Magdalene, and John. As Jesus looked down from the cross He was especially concerned for the welfare of His mother. He saw John, who He had great love and respect for. So in the moment of His death, He places the care of His mother into the hands of John the Apostle.

APPLICATION:

I don't think it is possible for us to really feel the emotional impact of the crucifixion on those who were there that day. But it is awesome to see the love Jesus had for people. He prayed for forgiveness of the soldiers. He gave forgiveness to the thief who was crucified beside Him. He showed love for His mother, and for John. The compassion Jesus possessed was without equal. Like someone has written, when we ask Jesus, "How much do You love us?" Jesus says, "This much," and He spreads His arms as wide as He can, and then has them nailed there!

VERSE TO MEMORIZE:
Galatians 6:14

Day 94

*Read –
John 19:28-37*

Those who crucified Jesus did not take His life, He gave it up of His own accord. In a prophetic statement, Jesus said in John 10:17-18, **"The reason My Father loves Me is that I lay down My life – only to take it up again. No one takes it from Me, but I lay it down of My own accord. I have authority to lay it down and authority to take it up again."** Jesus gave His life for you and me; it was not taken from Him: **"Jesus said, It is finished. With that, He bowed His head and gave up His spirit."**

Now, the Jews did not want the bodies of those crucified to remain on the cross over the Sabbath, so they requested that, if they weren't dead yet, their legs would be broken to hasten death. The soldiers came and broke the legs of the two crucified with Jesus, but when they came to Jesus, He was already dead. To make sure, one of the soldiers thrust his spear into the side of Jesus, which caused a mixture of blood and water to flow out. Some have stated that this is proof that Jesus died of a broken heart.

There on the cross that day two more scriptures were fulfilled. First of all, the rules regarding the killing of the sacrificial lamb for Passover were that no bones were to be broken. Numbers 9:11-12, **"They are to eat the lamb, together with unleavened bread and bitter herbs. They must not leave any of it till morning or break any of its bones. When they celebrate the Passover, they must follow all the regulations."** The second scripture is Zechariah 12:10, **"They will look on Me, the one they have pierced, and they will mourn for Him as one mourns for an only child, and grieve bitterly for Him as one grieves for a firstborn son."**

APPLICATION:

There is one thing that is obvious here: God was truly in charge. Everything that happened was a part of God's wonderful plan of redemption. The way Jesus died, the love He had for people, and the love that caused Him to willingly offer Himself as the supreme sacrifice for our sin. John 3:16 is so true: **"God so loved the world that He gave His one and only Son . . . "** Just for us!

VERSE TO MEMORIZE:
I John 3:1

Day 95

Read – John 19:38-42

Jesus had been crucified according to the great plan of God, Who in His love provided for our salvation through the death of Christ on the cross. Most of the disciples abandoned Him in His darkest hour. The only disciple we know who was at the cross is John. That's why John's account is so important to us; he was the only disciple who was actually an eyewitness to the events of the cross.

It is ironic that after Jesus had died, two men step forward to care for His lifeless body: Joseph of Arimathea and Nicodemus. Both of these men are members of the Sanhedrin, the Jewish ruling council. It was this very council that insisted that Jesus be put to death. Of course, Nicodemus was the one who had earlier come to Jesus at night and heard the words, **"You must be born again!"** Both he and Joseph had become secret followers of Jesus. But now Jesus is dead. They boldly go to Pilate and request the body of Jesus. Pilate grants their request. They took the body of Jesus, prepared it according to Jewish custom, and then laid the body in a brand-new tomb which was owned by Joseph.

I find it interesting that a man named Joseph played the supporting role at the birth of Jesus. And now, a man named Joseph plays a supporting role in the death of Jesus! And even though the disciples were not expecting it, Jesus didn't really need to use the tomb of Joseph for very long; He just needed to borrow it for the weekend!

APPLICATION:

There are so many times that in our humanness we do not understand the great plan of God. Even today, there are so many biblical scholars who try to help us understand what will happen at the end of the age. There are so many differing interpretations that we don't know what to believe. The Bible tells us in I Corinthians 2:9, **"No eye has seen, no ear has heard, no mind has conceived what God has prepared for those who love Him."** So let us simply trust, and allow God to be God in our lives.

VERSE TO MEMORIZE:
I Corinthians 2:9

Day 96

Read –
John 20:1-9

During His ministry Jesus had performed a real miracle in the life of Mary Magdalene. In Luke 8:2 we learn how Jesus cast seven demons out of her. She became a committed follower of Jesus. We see her at the cross, and now we see her early in the morning, on the first day of the week, making her way to the tomb to grieve for Jesus. It was still dark when she arrived at the tomb, and lo and behold, that huge stone that had sealed the tomb had been rolled away. She was shocked!

Immediately she ran to find Peter and John. When they heard her news they both took off running for the tomb. And John lets us know that he outran Peter. That would make a great trivia question: "Who was the faster man, Peter or John?" But though John got to the tomb first, he didn't go in. John bent over and viewed the grave clothes that were laying there. But when Peter arrived, he ran right on inside. He didn't stop at the entrance. That reflects Peter's personality. Both men observed the grave clothes laying there, and saw that the burial cloth that had been wrapped around Jesus' head was folded neatly – not likely if the body of Jesus had been stolen, as some have alleged.

Verses 8-9 are interesting to me: **"Finally the other disciple, who had reached the tomb first, also went inside. He saw and believed. (They still did not understand from Scripture that Jesus had to rise from the dead)."** This seems somewhat contradictory. They believed but still did not understand that He would rise from the dead. So what did they believe? Jesus had told these disciples at least three different times about what was going to happen to Him. But they had not understood.

APPLICATION:

Our faith is a progressive thing. What I believe today is so much greater than what I believed when I first met Jesus! Our faith is not a static faith, it is a dynamic faith. That was true for the disciples, and it is true for you and me. Paul prays for the faith of the Thessalonians in I Thessalonians 3:10, **"Night and day we pray most earnestly that we may see you again and supply what is lacking in your faith."** And then Paul thanks God that their faith is growing in II Thessalonians 1:3, **"We ought always to thank God for you, brothers,** and rightly so, because your faith is growing more and more, and the love every one of you has for each other is increasing."

VERSE TO MEMORIZE:
I John 5:4

Day 97

Read – John 20:10-18

John spends this whole section talking about Jesus' appearance to Mary Magdalene. He gives more attention here to Mary Magdalene than do any of the other gospel writers. Could it be because he and Mary Magdalene were at the cross together? Or because she is the first one to the tomb on Easter morning?

After meeting together at the empty tomb, Peter and John returned to their homes while Mary Magdalene stayed at the tomb and wept for the missing Jesus. As she did, she was confronted by two angels, who said to her, **"Why are you crying?"** She replied, **"They have taken my Lord away and I don't know where they have put Him."** Then she turned and saw Jesus, but didn't recognize Him. Could it be because of His glorified body, or maybe she was having difficulty seeing through her tears? She mistook Him for being the gardener. But when Jesus called her by name, all of a sudden, she knew Him. Can you imagine the feeling if we were to hear Jesus call our name!

Knowing that Jesus had truly risen from the grave, Mary Magdalene wanted to embrace Him. But Jesus said to her, **"Do not hold on to Me, for I have not yet returned to the Father. Go instead to My brothers and tell them, 'I am returning to My Father and your Father, to My God and your God.'"** Imagine the excitement when Mary found the disciples and said to them, **"I have seen the Lord!"**

APPLICATION:

Even though those early disciples experienced Jesus in a very physical way, our own experience of Jesus can be just as real. I love what John writes in his first epistle about the physical nature of their relationship with Jesus. John wrote, **"That which was from the beginning, which we have heard, which we have seen with our eyes, which we have looked at and our hands have touched – this we proclaim to you."** But at the same time when I read Mary Magdalene's words, **"I have seen the Lord,"** I too exclaim, "I have seen the Lord! Yes, I have truly seen the Lord!"

VERSE TO MEMORIZE:

I John 1:3

Day 98

Read – John 20:19-31

Imagine the scene; it is the evening on that first Sunday. The disciples have gathered together and are behind locked doors for fear of the Jews. They were probably discussing Mary Magdalene's claim that she has seen Jesus, when all of a sudden, Jesus was there in their midst. The locked doors did not keep Him out. In His glorified body He was no longer limited by time and space. His first words to them were, **"Peace be with you!"** In fact, He said it twice! They really needed peace at this point. It has been a rough weekend!

After pronouncing peace to the disciples, Jesus showed them His hands and side. The disciples were overjoyed! And then He commissioned them. He said to them, and ultimately to us, **"As the Father has sent Me, I am sending you."** And then He breathed on them and said, **"Receive the Holy Spirit."** The word for *spirit* actually means *breath*. We, too, need the breath of the Holy Spirit to flow through us. We can never take the gospel message to our world without it.

Jesus also commissioned His disciples that night with the authority to pronounce forgiveness to all who seek it.

One week later, the disciples were behind locked doors once again. This time Thomas was there. He had missed last week's meeting. When the disciples told him they had seen Jesus, His reply was, **"Unless I see the nail marks in His hands and put my finger where the nails were, and put my hand into His side, I will not believe it."** Jesus knew what Thomas had said, but He did not fault him for his words, rather He invited Thomas to do just what he said he needed to do in order to believe. It doesn't tell us that Thomas carried through on what he had said, but immediately Thomas said, **"My Lord and my God!"** And then Jesus spoke those words that are so important to us, **"Because you have seen Me, you have believed; blessed are those who have never seen and yet have believed."**

APPLICATION:

There are times in our humanness that we will have doubts. God understands that, and He does not condemn us for our doubts. He always wants to reassure us. Sin will separate us from God, but doubt never will as long as we take our doubts to Him.

VERSE TO MEMORIZE:

Isaiah 1:18

Day 99

Read –
John 21:1-14

In this passage Jesus invites seven of the disciples to join Him for breakfast. The story began the previous night. Jesus was not anywhere around, and Peter and six other disciples were bored. They knew Jesus was alive but they just didn't know what to do about it. So Peter said, **"I'm going fishing!"** The others said, **"We'll go with you."** They fished all night and caught nothing. On their way back to shore a man called out to them, **"Friends, have you caught anything?"** They answered in the negative. Then this man said, **"Throw your net on the right side of the boat and you will find some."** At this time they didn't know this was Jesus, but they had nothing to lose so they threw the net on the right side of the boat. Immediately the net filled with fish. About that time John said to Peter, **"It's the Lord!"**

When Peter realized it was Jesus he immediately jumped into the water and started swimming to shore. The fishing net was so full they had a hard time pulling it into the boat.

When they got to shore, Jesus said, **"Bring some of the fish you have just caught."** Jesus already had the fire going with some fish and bread on it. Their catch was such a big deal that they counted the fish they had caught. The Bible says there were 153 large fish.

When Jesus first called these fishermen to follow Him, He told them that from now on they would catch men. Now they had just heard Him say, **"As the Father has sent Me, I am sending you."** I wonder if they thought about any of that after this fishing miracle. That must have been some breakfast as they gathered around the fire with Jesus. And as Jesus took some bread and fish and gave it to them, I wonder if they were reminded once again of the feeding of the five thousand.

APPLICATION:

I don't know about you but I still believe God is in the miracle-working business. I've seen a few myself. I truly thank God that He has called me to be a fisher of men. It is truly a miracle when a person makes the decision to become a follower of Jesus. Jesus can perform any kind of miracle He wants to, but the most awesome of any miracle, is the miracle of a changed life!

VERSE TO MEMORIZE:
Mark 1:17

Day 100

Read – John 21:15-25

This passage recounts for us Jesus' reinstatement of Peter after his three denials. Just as Peter had denied Jesus three times, Jesus asks him three times, **"Simon, son of John, do you truly love Me more than these?"** Now it's hard to understand this dialogue without using the original Greek words that Jesus used. In the Greek language there are three different words for our word "Love." The first word is *Eros* from which we get the English word *Erotica*. That is love that is expressed for self-gratifying reasons like, "I love food" or "I love what pleasures me." The second word is the Greek word *Philia* which means *brotherly love*. I love you because you love me. It is a mutual love; shared with a friend. The third Greek word is the word *Agape* which is the word for divine love, or unconditional love. I love you in spite of any response I may receive from you.

When Jesus asks Peter the first two times if he loved Him, Jesus uses the word for divine love, *Agape*. But when Peter answers each time, he uses the word *Philia*, I love you because You love me. But the third time Jesus asks Peter He comes down to Peter's level with the word, *Philia*. In other words, "Peter, are you really My friend?" You see, the disciples never used the word for divine love until after the Holy Spirit was given to them on the Day of Pentecost. In our own humanness we are unable to love like God loves. But when He puts His Spirit in our hearts we are able to love like He wants us to love.

Now each time Jesus asked Peter if he loved Him, and Peter answered in the affirmative, Jesus gave him a mandate. He said to Peter, **"Feed My sheep"** or **"Care for My sheep."** Jesus ended this dialogue with the words, **"Follow Me!"** About that time Peter saw John following them, and he said to Jesus, **"Lord, what about him?"** Jesus responded, **"If I want him to remain alive until I return, what is that to you? You must follow Me."**

APPLICATION:

This passage is very applicable to every one of us. We have all failed Him at one time or another, but today His question to us is, "Do you really love Me? If you do, I want you to follow Me wherever I may lead you!" Failure never has to be final! Golfers have a saying: "It's not how you drive, it's how you arrive that counts." How true that is! How do you plan to arrive?

VERSE TO MEMORIZE:
Luke 9:62

An Acrostic Summary of John's Gospel

Following is an acrostic summary of every chapter in the gospel of John. The acrostic spells "John the gospel of belief." There are 21 letters, representing the 21 chapters of John's gospel. Every letter of the acrostic begins a summary sentence of what is in that chapter. This summary comes from Barry Huddleston's book, *The Acrostic Bible* (Thomas Nelson, Inc. Publishers 1978).

1 **J**esus is the Word
2 **O**utstanding miracle at Cana
3 **H**eavenly birth taught Nicodemus
4 **N**eed of Samaritan woman

5 **T**estimony to Jesus' deity
6 **H**oly Bread of life
7 **E**xclamation at the feast

8 **G**race for adulteress defended
9 **O**pposition to removing blindness
10 **S**hepherd and His sheep
11 **P**ower to raise Lazarus

12 Entry into Jerusalem triumphant
13 Last supper and discourse

14 **O**ffer of the Holy Spirit
15 Fruit of the vine

16 **B**eliever's comfort and joy
17 Extended prayer of Christ
18 Lord's betrayal and denial
19 Illegal trials and crucifixion
20 Eyewitnesses to the resurrection
21 Final charge to Peter

List of Scriptures for Memorization

Joshua 24:15	Matthew 5:16	John 1:14
I Samuel 16:17	Matthew 6:33	John 2:5
Psalms 5:11	Matthew 28:18-20	John 2:17
Psalms 9:10	Mark 1:17	John 2:24-25
Psalms 19:14	Luke 9:62	John 3:3
Psalms 40:12-13	Romans 1:16	John 3:16
Psalms 86:5	Romans 1:20	John 3:36
Psalms 119:9	Romans 6:23	John 4:13-14
Psalms 119:11	Romans 8:28	John 4:42
Psalms 119:169	Romans 10:9-10	John 5:24
Psalms 145:9	Romans 12:2	John 5:39
Proverbs 3:5-6	Romans 15:13	John 6:35
Proverbs 11:3	I Corinthians 2:2	John 8:12
Proverbs 28:1	I Corinthians 2:4-5	John 10:10
Ecclesiastes 9:10	I Corinthians 2:9	John 10:14
Isaiah 1:18	I Corinthians 2:13	John 10:30
Isaiah 55:8	I Corinthians 13:12	John 14:2-3
Jeremiah 29:13	II Corinthians 10:3-4	John 14:6-7
	Galatians 4:6-7	John 14:26

Galatians 6:14	John 14:27
Ephesians 1:7-8	John 15:5
Colossians 1:28-29	John 15:13
Colossians 3:17	John 15:16
I Timothy 1:8	John 16:33
II Timothy 4:7-8	John 17:3
Titus 3:3-5	John 17:15-16
Hebrews 11:6	John 17:22-23
Hebrews 12:25	John 20:30-31
Hebrews 13:6	I John 1:3
James 1:5	I John 3:1
James 2:14	I John 5:4
I Peter 2:9	I John 5:14-15
I Peter 2:21	III John 2
Revelation 3:20	III John 4
Revelation 12:11	
Revelation 21:6	
Revelation 22:7	

www.ingramcontent.com/pod-product-compliance
Lightning Source LLC
Chambersburg PA
CBHW030320100526
44592CB00010B/503